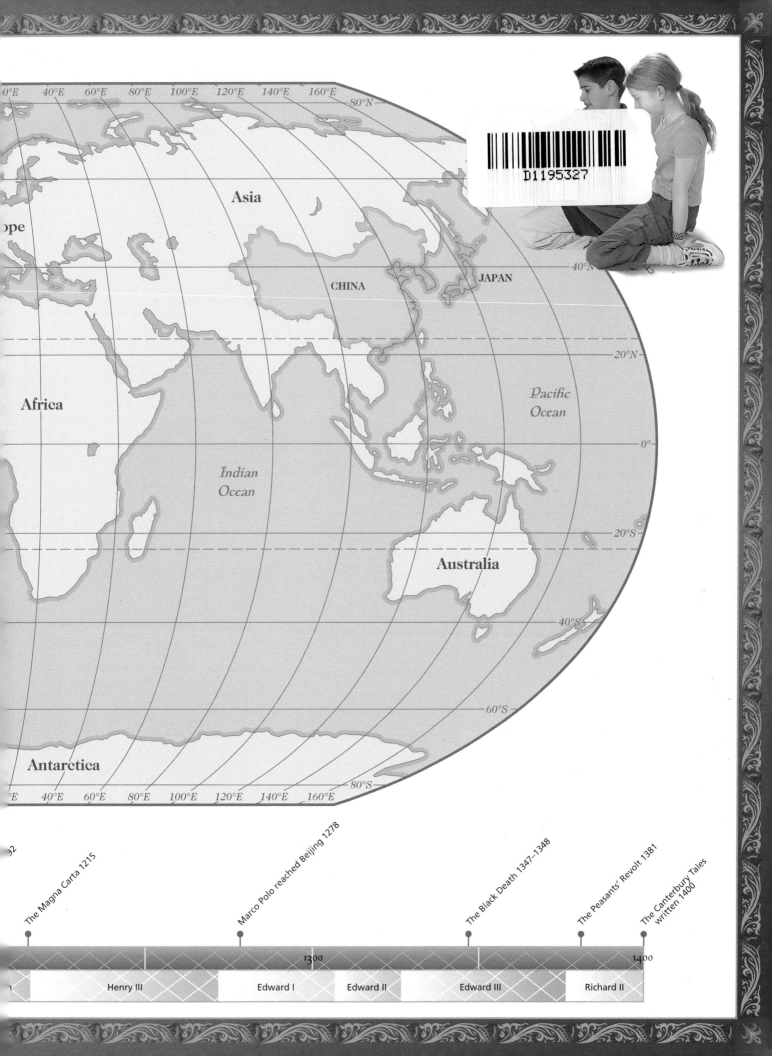

40°E 60°E 80°E 100°E 120°E 140°E 160°E 80°N

ope

Asia

40°N

CHINA JAPAN

20°N

Africa

Pacific
Ocean

Indian
Ocean

0°

20°S

Australia

40°S

60°S

Antarctica

80°S

40°E 60°E 80°E 100°E 120°E 140°E 160°E

The Magna Carta 1215

Marco Polo reached Beijing 1278

The Black Death 1347–1348

The Peasants' Revolt 1381

The Canterbury Tales
written 1400

1300   1400

Henry III   Edward I   Edward II   Edward III   Richard II

Medieval Times

Mary Nelson

DUVAL HOUSE
PUBLISHING
LES ÉDITIONS DUVAL

Duval House Publishing Inc.

18228 – 102 Avenue
Edmonton, Alberta T5S 1S7
Ph: 1-800-267-6187
Fax: (780) 482-7213
Website: http://www.duvalhouse.com

Author

Mary Nelson

National Library of Canada Cataloguing in Publication Data

Nelson, Mary, 1937-
 Medieval times

Includes index.
ISBN 1-55220-203-8

1. Civilization, Medieval—Juvenile literature. 2. Great Britain—History—Medieval period, 1066-1485—Juvenile literature. I. Title.
D118.N44 2002   940.1   C2002-910408-4

Project Team

Project managers: Karen Iversen, Betty Gibbs

Editors: Betty Gibbs, Karen Iversen, Shauna Babiuk

Cover and text design: Claudia Bordeleau (Obsidian Multimedia)

Photo research: David Strand

Production: Claudia Bordeleau, Leslie Stewart, Jeff Miles

Maps and illustrations: Johnson Cartographics Inc., Wendy Johnson; Claudia Bordeleau, Lorna Bennett, Chao Yu and Jue Wang, Don Hight

Photographer: New Visions Photography (Brad Callihoo)

Photo shoot coordinator: Roberta Wildgoose

Manufacturers

Screaming Colour Inc., Quality Color Press

Photographic Models

Grace Fung
Said Hamdon
Adrian Osman
Katy Wilfong-Pritchard

Validators

Educational

Dolores Cascone
Curriculum Resource Teacher
Toronto Catholic District School Board

Sandee Elliott, Teacher
Muirhead Elementary School
Toronto, Ontario

Patricia Elliott, B.Ed., M.A., Resource Teacher
Simcoe County District School Board
Midhurst, Ontario

Bias Reviewer

Kennard Ramphal
Scarborough Centre for Alternative Studies
Toronto District School Board
Scarborough, Ontario

Historical

Margot Mortensen, MA
Humanities Department
Grant MacEwan Community College
Edmonton, Alberta

Many website addresses have been identified in this textbook. These are provided as suggestions and are not intended to be a complete resource list. Duval House Publishing does not guarantee that these websites will not change or continue to exist. Duval House does not endorse the content of the website nor any websites linked to the site. You should consult with your teacher whenever using Internet resources.

We acknowledge the financial support of the Government of Canada through the Book Publishing Industry Development Program for our publishing activities.

Canada

Printed and bound in Canada

First Printing

Acknowledgements

The author sincerely acknowledges and thanks the many people involved in the creation of this book. Thank you to Karen Iversen of Duval House, who gave me the opportunity to experience this exciting project. Without her vision, knowledge, and encouragement this book would not have been produced. Thank you to Betty Gibbs for her hours of editing and her willing collaboration, and to David Strand, who tirelessly pursued sources for the medieval artwork and artifacts in the book. Thanks to Claudia Bordeleau for her exciting book design and graphics, and to Chao Yu and Jue Wang, Lorna Bennett, and Don Hight for the thoughtful and expressive illustrations that accompany the text, lending life to the words. Wendy Johnson's clear and attractive maps aid in the presentation of the time period. To the student models, photographer, and all others involved, I also say thank you. My understanding of producing a book has changed considerably.

To the staff of the Calgary Public Library, and in particular those at the Louise Riley Branch, thank you for your help in tracking down ideas and for the endless renewals. I thank my family, Gordon, Craig and Daniel, Laura, Bernie, and Clara, and my friends, for their patient support and encouragement in all the stages of this project.

To The Student

Most of you already know some things about medieval times. There are stories, movies, and even video games about knights, castles, lords, and ladies. However, there is much more you can learn about the medieval period of history.

Different groups of people had quite different lives. In this textbook, you will look at medieval villages and the lives of farming and working people. Next you will study a medieval castle and see what life was like for a noble family and for all the other people who lived in a castle. From the castle, you will go to a town and meet townspeople. Then you will look at rulers and other people at the royal court.

Religion was important in medieval times. This textbook looks at Christianity and Islam, including ways they have influenced lives today.

People today have inherited many legacies from the past. That means things have been passed down to us from people who lived long ago. Some of them will surprise you. Watch for pieces of information marked "Legacy" as you read the textbook.

Pieces of information marked "Elsewhere..." will give snapshots of life in various places in the world during the same time period.

Medieval Times has many different sources of information for you to use in your learning. There are illustrations, photos, maps, charts, graphs, and stories, as well as text information. The glossary on pages 135 to 138 defines new words for you. The index at the back of the textbook will help you locate information in it. Use the maps inside the front and back covers of the textbook for quick reference to places you are studying.

You will work on a medieval project throughout this study. It focuses on both learning and fun.

In this textbook, four Canadian children invite you to learn new skills and get involved in hands-on projects. I hope you enjoy your trip into the past with them!

Contents

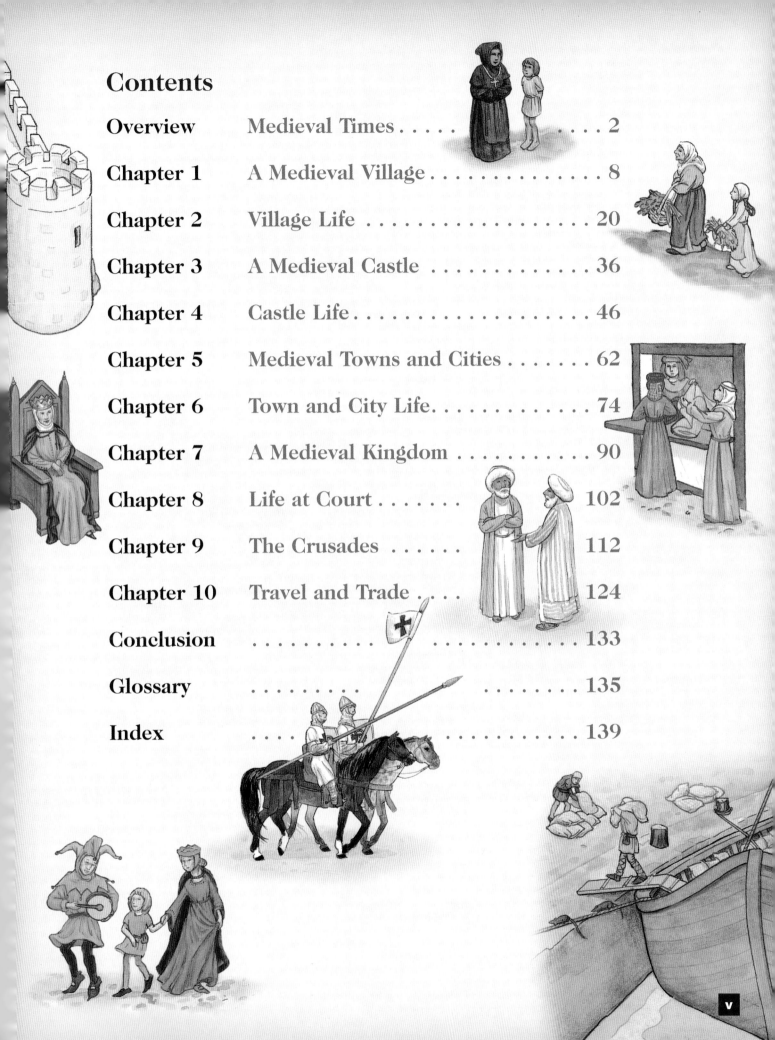

Medieval Times

Castles, kings, queens, knights, lords, and ladies were all part of a colourful time in history called the medieval period. So were farm workers, inn-keepers, nuns, and many others. Together, let's follow a winding route through village, castle, town, and kingdom. Then we will travel over sea and land to learn about Islam, the Crusades, trade, and a terrible disease called plague, on our journey through medieval times.

Medieval Times Project

Creating a Medieval Times Board Game

As you study *Medieval Times*, you will find ideas and information. Use these, and your imagination, to help create a Medieval Times Board Game.

You will work on your project in groups of 4 or 5. Each group will design and construct a board game that can be played, displayed, and presented to others.

1. Each group should start a game folder to organize and store its work. Agree on a name for your group, label your folder with it, put your group members' names on the folder, and find a space to keep it.

You will gather and organize ideas and create your game as you learn. Throughout the textbook, you will be given reminders and suggestions for completing your board game.

Predictions from Images

Making predictions about what you expect to find out in a textbook helps you to learn. Predictions are statements about what is likely to happen in the future. The images (illustrations and photographs) are linked to the written information. Look at images (for example, pages 2 and 3) for clues to predict what the written information will be about.

1. Create a prediction chart for recording your prediction statements.

2. Look at the image as a whole. Ask yourself:
   - Where is it? What is the environment like?
   - When is it? Is it in the past, present, or future?

Topic:		
What I think I will learn	Evidence to support prediction	What I found out
Details I don't understand		

3. Look at the activity and the details in the image. Ask yourself:
   - If there are people or characters, who are they? What do their clothes tell you about them?
   - How do the characters behave towards each other?
   - What actions are going on?
   - What types of technology, such as tools and methods of doing things, are shown?

4. Write predictions about what you think you will learn in the first column of your chart.

5. In the second column, note the evidence in the picture that supports your predictions.

6. Note any details you don't understand at the bottom of the chart.

7. When you have finished reading the information, write down what you found out in the third column of the chart. Compare it to the predictions.

Do ◊ Discuss ◊ Discover

1. Examine the image on pages 2 and 3. Follow the steps below to predict what this textbook will be about.

   a) Make a chart with space for 5 predictions. Write down your prediction statements and evidence, and note any details you cannot explain.

   b) Put your chart in your notebook. You will look at it again after you finish Chapter 10 to confirm or correct your predictions.

Studying History

History is the study of people and events of the past. In this textbook, you will look at the history of some people and events between the years 1000 and 1400 CE (Common Era). The textbook will focus on the history of England. You will also look at people and events in history elsewhere around the world.

The maps in this textbook show the locations of places you will read about. There are larger maps inside the front and back covers that show how different places relate to each other.

The United Kingdom

This map shows the United Kingdom and some nearby countries in Europe today. Some of these countries existed in medieval times. The boundaries of most of them have changed. See the map on the left inside the back cover for boundaries in medieval times.

Studying a Society

All of the people living in a place at a certain time make up the **society**. Historians look at different groups of people in a society. Social groups can be compared in many different ways. Here are some useful ways:

- the ways they met their needs for houses, food, clothing, and health

- the roles and occupations of the members

- the kinds of technology (tools, weapons, ideas for solving problems)

- the more and less important, wealthy, or powerful social groups

- the rights and responsibilities of members of social groups

- the ways social groups were organized and governed

- their religion and beliefs

In this textbook, you will study different groups that lived in medieval times. The list above will help you compare them.

Medieval Society

In medieval society, groups had different rank based on their power, wealth, and land they controlled. The king had the highest rank. **Nobles** were the strongest, most important lords and their families.

Nobles were **vassals** of the king or of other nobles. Vassals promised loyalty, certain services, and taxes to their lord. In return, the vassal received control of some land and the income it produced.

The king ruled the whole country and received taxes and support from the nobles.

In this book, "the Church" refers to the Roman Catholic Church.

Nobles and important leaders in the Church controlled most of the land of the country. Their landholdings were called **manors**. Most nobles were also **knights**. They were vassals of the king.

Less powerful nobles (lords) and knights were given land in return for their loyalty and support. They promised to supply fighting men and money when the ruler needed it.

Freemen and freewomen worked as craftspeople, worked for wages, or farmed plots of land. They paid rent and taxes to a lord. They could move to other manors or towns to find work.

Serfs farmed nobles' land. They worked in a lord's fields and gave the lord part of the produce from their small fields. The men could be asked to fight in wars. The lord gave them protection from attack and a place to live and work. It was difficult for serfs to leave the manor.

Making a Social Pyramid

You will need

- construction paper
- pencil, ruler, scissors
- masking tape
- pencil crayons, felts

A pyramid has triangles for sides and a square bottom. It is a very strong, solid structure that doesn't crush easily. The largest area is at the bottom, which supports the area above it.

Work in pairs to do this activity.

1. Draw the pattern **A** onto a piece of construction paper, using the measurements provided here. Then cut it out.

2. Create a diagram of the medieval social structure on your pyramid. Write the categories shown on page 6 on one side of the pyramid. Make small illustrations of people from the different groups at the correct levels on a second side.

3. Fold the sides and the flap along the dotted lines. Lightly tape the flap to the far side with masking tape to form the pyramid, **B**.

4. Put your pyramid in a safe place. You will refer to it again in later chapters.

A

12 cm 12 cm 12 cm 12 cm

18 cm 18 cm 18 cm 18 cm

Fold on dotted lines

18 cm 2.1 cm 15.5 cm 1.5 cm

B

ruler

nobles (barons) bishops

lesser nobles ladies abbots/abbesses knights

merchants artisans freemen/freewomen

serfs serfs serfs serfs serfs

Do ◆ Discuss ◆ Discover

1. Begin a Vocabulary section in your notebook. Create a title page and/or a divider to mark it. Add the terms printed in red on pages 5 and 6 to your Vocabulary section. Explain each term in your own words. You will add to this section throughout your study.

Chapter 1
A Medieval Village

During medieval times, hundreds of small villages dotted the countryside. These villages belonged to large manors controlled by lords. Farm workers called serfs lived in small houses. Villages usually included the lord's manor house, a church, and a mill for grinding flour from grain. Farm fields surrounded the village.

Focus on Learning

In this chapter you will learn about
- types of medieval villages
- village houses
- other village buildings
- fields, forests, and streams

Vocabulary

common	linen
pasture	great hall
ford	forge
abbey	open field system
wattle and daub	fallow
thatched roof	poacher

Medieval Villages

Most villages were surrounded by farm fields. Small houses were clustered together, and paths zigzagged among them.

Many villages had a central green space called a **common**. The villagers used the common as a shared **pasture**. Their own animals fed on the grass. The lord's animals were in a separate pasture.

Some medieval villages were built near or even inside the walls of a castle that belonged to the lord of the manor. The castle protected the serfs and other village people in time of war.

Some villages were built where two roads crossed, or near a **ford** or bridge. A ford was a shallow place in a river where people and animals could cross.

Rievaulx Abbey in northern England was a huge complex, as can be seen from these ruins.

Very large manors had many villages, each with surrounding fields. A wealthy lord often gave control of part of his land to a knight.

Some manors belonged to the Church. The serfs on those manors gave part of their crop to an **abbey**, where a religious community of monks lived.

Small manors were often called "one knight's fee" because they provided a knight's income.

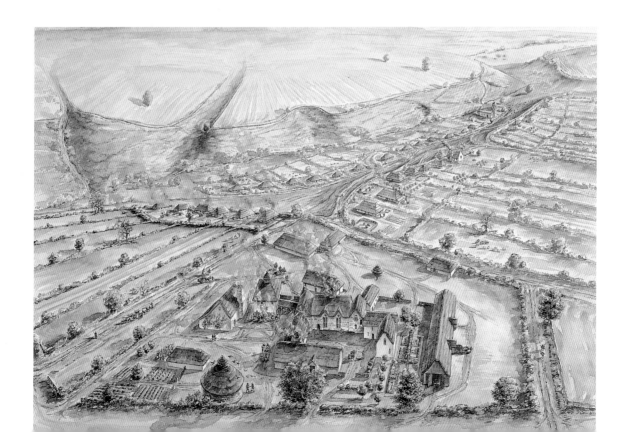

Village Houses

Some medieval villages had fewer than one hundred people living in a cluster of houses. Large villages might have several hundred people.

A whole family ate, slept, and lived together in a village house. Most houses were small—12 to 15 metres long and 3 to 4 metres wide. They had only one or two rooms.

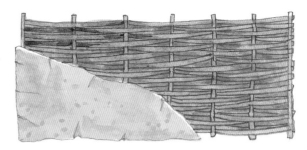

To make **wattle and daub**, thin branches were woven together and then placed between support beams. The woven branches were plastered with a mixture of clay, dung, and straw.

Thatched roofs could last for about 20 years before being replaced.

thatched roof made of thick layers of straw or reeds tied onto the roof frame

hole in the roof for smoke to escape— no chimney

wooden ridgepole beam holding up the roof

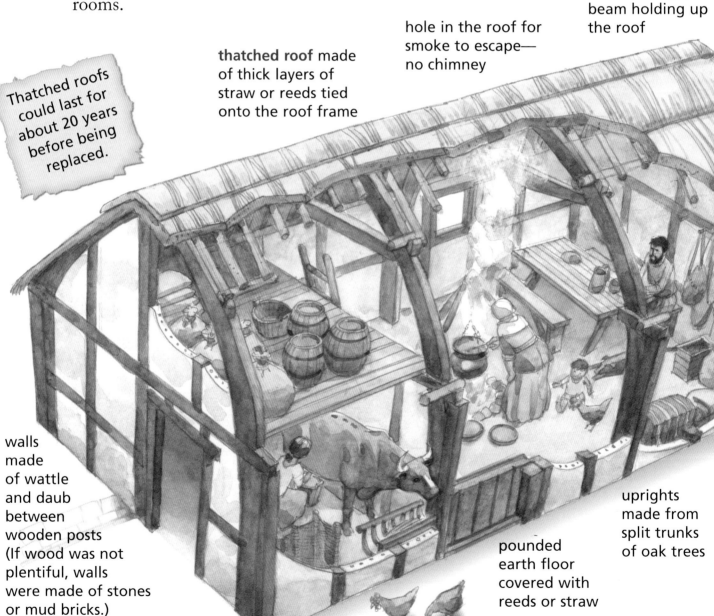

walls made of wattle and daub between wooden posts (If wood was not plentiful, walls were made of stones or mud bricks.)

pounded earth floor covered with reeds or straw

uprights made from split trunks of oak trees

wooden corner posts resting on a foundation or in a trench

Inside a Village House

There was little furniture in a serf's or freeman's house, compared to most houses today. Furnishings were hand-made from wood or other materials from the environment.

There were simple, strong wooden trestle tables, stools, and benches. People slept on mattresses made of cloth bags filled with straw or sheep's wool. These were laid on the floor at night.

Most people used woolen blankets or animal hides for their bed coverings. The wealthiest people had woven **linen** sheets. Linen is a cloth made from the fibres in the stem of the flax plant.

Dry reeds dipped in animal fat were burned to provide light. A fire-pit in the centre of the floor was used for cooking. It also provided light and warmth.

Belongings and clothes were stored in a chest or hung on pegs.

Homes had no running water, bathrooms, or indoor toilets. Water was carried in leather buckets from the community well. People used a public latrine trench as a toilet. Otherwise, they went a distance from the cottage to relieve themselves.

Villagers grew vegetables in their backyard gardens for food.

Animals often shared space with people at night. This kept them safe from predators and thieves. The animals' body heat helped to keep the family warm in winter. Families with larger houses sometimes kept the animals in a separate room or a fenced yard.

Windows

In the poorest houses, windows were small holes in the wall. These were covered with shutters at night to keep out the cold.

Some people covered frames in cloth soaked in fat and resin from tree sap to cover windows. These let in a little light. They could be removed when the weather was nice.

A few people had windows covered with thin slices of polished horn. These let in light but were not transparent.

Only very wealthy people could afford glass. Even for them, glass was difficult to get.

Do ◆ Discuss ◆ Discover

1. Discuss with a partner the safety hazards in a village house. List three concerns in your notebook.
2. The materials used to build a cottage all came from the environment. Make a chart with two columns. List the parts of a village house and the source of the materials.

Making a Village House

You will need

- lightweight cardboard
- tan/yellow paper
- 6 small wooden craft sticks
- 4 jumbo wooden craft sticks
- scissors, pencil, ruler
- white glue
- masking tape
- brown felt pens
- white paint

C 4 cm 6 cm
Roof supports
(Make 3)
8 cm

D 15 cm

16 cm
B (Cut 13) 2 cm 6 cm 6 cm

7 cm **A** (Cut 2)
1 cm 15 cm 8 cm

1. Measure and draw the pattern pieces shown here. Cut two side/end pieces (**A**) from cardboard and 13 strips (**B**) from paper.

2. Paint the side/end pieces white. Draw and colour wooden beams, supports, and window and door frames. Cut out windows and a door.

3. To make the walls, score along the dotted lines of the side/end pieces and fold. Glue the corner tab of each piece to the end of the other piece to form a rectangle.

4. Cut six pieces 6 cm long and three pieces 4 cm long from the small wooden craft sticks. With masking tape, make three A-shaped roof supports, as shown in **C**. Assemble and tape or glue together the roof frame using the jumbo sticks and the roof supports, as shown in **D**.

5. Use the paper to make roof thatch. Fold *one* strip of paper in half lengthwise. With scissors, make small cuts along both sides. Do not cut through the middle. On all other strips, cut longer fringes along one side, joined at the other edge. Glue six strips of "thatch" to each side of the roof frame. Begin at the bottom edge and overlap each strip. Glue the single folded strip along the peak of the roof.

6. Cut a cardboard base large enough to support your house. This will form the floor. Draw a hearth fire in the middle of it. Place the walls on the base and set the roof on top of the walls.

Other Village Buildings

Medieval villages usually had a manor house for the lord's use, a church, and at least one mill.

The Manor House

The manor house was used by the lord of the manor. It was larger and better constructed than village houses. It was often built out of stone for strength and beauty. It had more rooms, more windows, and more space around it.

There were gardens for food and herbs around the manor house. Out-buildings for animals and storage were part of the complex. A wall usually surrounded the whole manor house complex.

A wealthy lord who had other houses only used the manor house when he visited the village. A less important noble or a knight might live in it with his family most of the time.

The manor house usually had a large room called the **great hall**. It could be used for meetings, celebrations, and special events. The villagers attended special events like a Christmas banquet in the great hall.

This medieval great hall holds a display of historical objects.

Do ◊ Discuss ◊ Discover

1. Review pages 10 to 13. Gather information from the images and text about village houses and manor houses.

   a) Work with a partner to find and discuss the similarities and differences.

   b) Record your notes in a graphic organizer in your notebook.

The Village Church

The village church and the manor house were the largest buildings in the village. Churches were often made of wood at first. As a village grew larger, the church was rebuilt from stone. The church was often enclosed by a wall to keep farm animals out.

In medieval times, this church would not have had these wooden seats. People stood or knelt on the stone floors to pray.

The medieval wall around this churchyard is no longer standing.

Churches commonly contained carved figures of saints. Some showed brightly painted scenes from the Bible on the walls. The Bible is the holy book of Christians. Most villagers could not read, so images were important for teaching about Christianity. (You will read more about this on page 31.)

Elsewhere...

This wooden church in Vik, Norway, was built around 1200. It is one of the oldest churches of its kind in Norway.

Other Structures

Some parts of a medieval village were shared by the community. These buildings were usually built at the lord's expense. People paid in goods or money for these services.

People brought their loaves of bread to be baked in a shared oven or a bakeshop.

A blacksmith's **forge** held a hot fire for heating metal. The blacksmith made tools and metal objects. He shoed horses for the villagers.

Today, most people buy their bread. It is made with machines and baked in huge ovens.

Flour mills might be powered by moving water or wind. The motion turned the huge grindstones, which ground grain into flour.

Do ◊ Discuss ◊ Discover

1. With a partner, discuss the advantages of some services being shared in the community. Identify 3 services in your community that are shared by people, and explain why.

2. Look at the activity and details in the flour mill image on the left. List the numbered activities in the order they would have occurred. Explain each step.

The Fields

The land belonging to the manor was farmed by the serfs and freemen who lived in the village.

Villagers grew grain crops (wheat, barley, oats, and rye) for flour and fields of beans and peas.

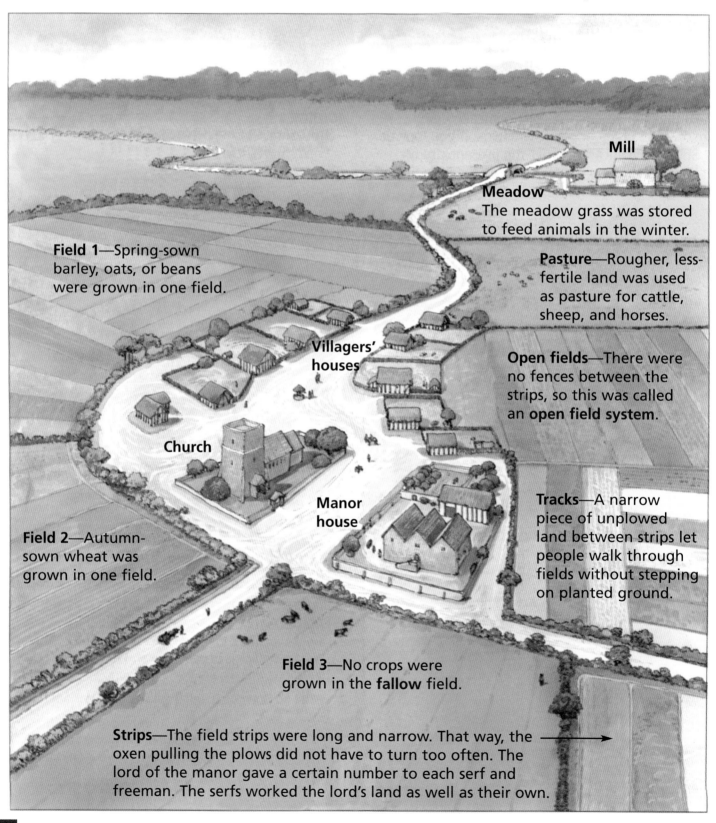

Mill

Meadow—The meadow grass was stored to feed animals in the winter.

Field 1—Spring-sown barley, oats, or beans were grown in one field.

Pasture—Rougher, less-fertile land was used as pasture for cattle, sheep, and horses.

Villagers' houses

Open fields—There were no fences between the strips, so this was called an **open field system**.

Church

Manor house

Tracks—A narrow piece of unplowed land between strips let people walk through fields without stepping on planted ground.

Field 2—Autumn-sown wheat was grown in one field.

Field 3—No crops were grown in the **fallow** field.

Strips—The field strips were long and narrow. That way, the oxen pulling the plows did not have to turn too often. The lord of the manor gave a certain number to each serf and freeman. The serfs worked the lord's land as well as their own.

Crop Rotation

Medieval farmers usually grew a different crop each year in two of the main fields. The third field was fallow. Fallow fields were not planted with a crop for one year out of three. The soil was allowed to rest. Animals grazed on any plants that grew in the fallow field.

Always growing the same crop in a field used up soil nutrients quickly. Changing the crop and fallowing a field produced more grain. The villagers had to agree about what to grow and which field to leave fallow each year.

	Year 1	Year 2	Year 3
Field 1	Wheat	Oats	....
Field 2	Oats	Fallow	....
Field 3	Fallow	Wheat	....

Fertilizer

Manure was used as fertilizer. In the winter, all sheep had to be pastured in the lord's pasture area. Sheep manure was valuable and belonged to the lord.

The stream providing water for the village often flowed through fields and pastures. Animal waste could pollute the water supply.

In countries like Canada, farms today are much larger than medieval farms. Farmers use many types of power machinery. They are able to work more quickly and use fewer farm workers. Fields are larger. Many farms still use crop rotation to keep their land productive.

There are new types of crops today that yield more produce. Chemical and natural fertilizers are used to add nutrients to the soil. Pesticides are used to kill weeds and insects.

Farmers today still worry about crops failing. Disease, insects, bad weather, drought, and floods still affect crops. Farmers are also concerned about pollution of water and soil. When soil and water are damaged, they take a long time to recover.

Do ◊ Discuss ◊ Discover

1. Sketch an imaginary village with its three fields. Use the illustration on page 16 to help. Mark on the sketch the way the fields would be used in Year 3 of the chart shown on this page.

2. Discuss ways the water of a medieval village might be polluted.

Forests and Streams

Sometimes there was a forest near the village. Forests and the animals living in them belonged to the king. The lord of the manor often had permission from the king to use the forest near the manor. Then the lord controlled the amount of kindling (dry wood), nuts, and other forest products the villagers could use.

The natural forests in most of England and northern Europe are hardwood trees. Hardwood trees such as oak have strong, straight trunks. The wood resists rotting. Hardwood makes excellent building material.

In medieval times, huge trees were needed to make the beams in roofs of churches, abbeys, manor houses, and castles.

There were forests of oak, beech, and elm trees hundreds of years old. Few of these natural forests remain today. They were cut down for building and to clear land for farming. Some forests have been replanted.

Medieval forests were the habitat of many kinds of animals and birds. Hunting was a favourite sport of kings, queens, and nobles. It was against the law for anyone else to kill animals of the woodland. **Poachers** who were caught hunting or fishing illegally were punished.

Fishing rights belonged to the lord. Villagers had to pay a fee if they wished to take fish from a stream. One fishing method was to set fish traps made from woven branches in the flowing stream.

Using Your Learning

Understanding Concepts

1. List two advantages and two disadvantages of having the hearth fire in the middle of a village home.

2. Examine the illustration on page 18. Identify three activities that demonstrate how the forests and streams were used in medieval times.

3. Identify vocabulary from this chapter to add to the Vocabulary section of your notebook, which you started on page 7. Add diagrams or sketches to help you remember the words and their meanings.

Developing Inquiry/Research and Communication Skills

4. Go to http://loki.stockton.edu/~ken/wharram/wharram.htm. Write notes about the abandoned medieval village from information provided in diagrams, photographs, and evidence on this website. Share your notes with a classmate.

Applying Skills and Concepts in Various Contexts

5. a) Create a poster illustrating causes of pollution in a medieval village and in a modern Canadian town or city.

   b) Write a short summary describing similarities and differences.

6. Review pages 5 and 6. People from more than one social group lived in a village. Discuss with a partner, and predict, which social groups lived in or used the different buildings in a village.

Medieval Times Project

1. With your group, collect a variety of board games from school and home. Look at them for ideas of types of board games.

2. Discuss board games you have seen or played. Read and discuss the instructions to the games. The game that you are going to make should be fun to play and also help you and other players learn about medieval times. Think about and discuss how you can include learning in a board game.

3. With your group, review Chapter 1. Write four questions and answers that identify key information about medieval villages. This information may be used in different ways, depending on the design of your game. Keep the questions and answers in your game folder. You will add more in each chapter.

Chapter 2
Village Life

Life in a medieval village was seldom quiet. Dogs barked, the mill wheel creaked, and the blacksmith's hammer clanged. Everyone was busy outdoors most of the time. Most people worked in the fields, but villages also had craftspeople, managers, and a village priest.

Focus on Learning

In this chapter you will learn about
- how the villagers met their basic needs for food and clothing
- what health care was like
- the farm work of a village
- other occupations of villagers
- religion in medieval times
- the village priest and education
- village justice
- asking questions

Vocabulary

self-sufficient	reeve
staple foods	Domesday Book
distaff	shrine
weaver	penance
apothecary	tithe
steward	manorial court
bailiff	stocks

Food

Medieval villages were almost **self-sufficient**. That means the villagers met most of their basic needs from their farms. Some other products came from the natural environment.

All of the **staple foods** were grown in their gardens and fields. Staple foods are the basic foods eaten every day. Vegetables, grains, and dairy products were the basic foods. Peas and beans added protein to the diet. Dried peas and beans were boiled for pease porridge or added to stews. Meat was eaten on special occasions. Chickens that no longer laid eggs were eaten.

Herbs	
parsley	borage
mint	watercress
fennel	rosemary
garlic	rue
sage	purslane

Herbs were used to flavour vegetable stews. Honey was the only sweetener available.

Starvation was sometimes a threat. If there was a poor harvest, people often died. People also got sick when they did not have enough of the right kinds of food.

Drink

Village water supplies were commonly polluted and not safe to drink.

Ale brewed from barley was an important part of the diet because it provided nutrition. Brewing purified the water used to make the ale.

Metal cooking cauldrons on legs stood right in the hearth fire.

Women often made a small income for their families by making ale to sell.

bread

pease porridge

milk

cheese

bacon
dried peas
and beans

herbs

cabbage

eggs

leeks

onions

Breakfast:
Bread and ale

Lunch (in the fields):
Bread, ale, cheese, or
meat if available

Supper:
Vegetable stew,
bread, ale

Clothing

The villagers made their clothing from wool, tanned leather, and sheepskin.

A man with more wealth might own a linen shirt for special occasions. Some women had a linen underdress called a shift.

Men and women often wore a hood over their head and shoulders called a capuchin.

People wore either wooden clogs or heavy leather coverings tied around their feet.

Children wore a smaller, shorter version of adult clothing.

Women made wool thread from sheep's wool. Short fibres of wool were twisted together to make a continuous thread. The common technology for spinning thread was a **distaff**. The woman twirled a rod to twist the thread. Spinning wheels were more common after 1300.

Some women also made the cloth for their family's clothing. However, most women traded their spun thread to **weavers** for some of the cloth they made. Weavers were craftspeople who made and sold cloth.

Dyes made from local plants were used to colour cloth. For example, onion skins made a yellow-brown dye. Dark colours were practical for the hard-working village people.

Do ◆ Discuss ◆ Discover

1. Review the information on pages 20–22.
   a) Write 2–3 sentences in your notebook about medieval villagers' food.
   b) Write 2–3 sentences about their clothing.

Health

Villagers needed to be strong for their busy outdoor working life. However, illness and injury were common. The average length of life was fairly short in medieval times. Many babies, new mothers, and young children died.

Few people knew what caused illnesses or how to treat them. Doctors were not common in villages. Village women who understood herbal medicines were called healers. They grew herbs or gathered them from the environment.

Feverfew was used for headache and to help in childbirth.

Village women helped each other in childbirth and tended sick people. Sometimes a village would have a midwife. Midwives helped other women have babies.

The flowers and leaves of yarrow were made into a medicinal tea.

A healer might suggest certain types of food and drink, exercise, or rest. Prayers for the sick were often part of treating illness.

Healers also needed to know how to set broken bones and treat wounds. A hot iron was used to cauterize (seal off) a bleeding wound.

Villagers who lived near a monastery or convent could sometimes get help from the monks or nuns. Some religious communities had an **apothecary**. Apothecaries were specially trained in making medicines.

One of the uses of comfry was to help heal broken bones.

Do ◊ Discuss ◊ Discover

1. Discuss with a partner how health was connected to the environment.

Farm Work

Every day was a working day in the village, except Sundays, feast days, or holy days. Some farm chores, like milking cows and feeding animals, had to be done every day. People got up at sunrise and worked until dark. Then they ate supper and went to bed.

Families worked in the fields together, especially at planting and harvest time. Young children worked at tasks like clearing stones from fields or feeding animals. Babies were swaddled, which means they were wrapped up tight. They could be hung from a branch or left beside a field while parents worked.

When the crops on the manor were ready to harvest, everyone had to help. They harvested the lord of the manor's crops first. Then they cut their own grain.

SPRING
- plow fields
- clear stones
- plant crops
- prune fruit trees
- shear sheep

SUMMER
- tend animals
- weed gardens/fields
- harvest fall-planted grain
- pick fruit

WINTER
- repair fences, tools, buildings

AUTUMN
- thresh grain
- take pigs to forest to eat nuts
- plant fall grain crops
- store hay for winter
- slaughter pigs
- smoke and salt meat

Year-round Work

- make cheese
- brew ale
- spin thread
- garden
- milk cows and goats
- keep chickens
- prepare food
- care for children

Images of Village Farm Life

The image on the right is a stained-glass window. The three images below come from medieval books. Books were copied and illustrated by hand. Decorations and small images filled any spaces where there was no text. No space was wasted. Books were usually about religious subjects. Pictures sometimes showed scenes from daily life.

This farm youth is scattering seeds of grain onto the field around him.

This woman, who is feeding a hen and chicks, carries a distaff under her arm.

Cows were usually milked by women.

At harvest time, everyone in the village had to help cut and bundle the ripe grain before rain could spoil it.

Do ◊ Discuss ◊ Discover

1. As a class, discuss how the four images above illustrate the daily lives of villagers.

2. Divide a blank page into four. Label each section a different season. Draw/Illustrate a farm activity in each season. Write a sentence about each activity.

Craftspeople

Some people in the village were not farm workers. They provided services and made products for the villagers and the lord. They were often paid in food or farm products.

Craftspeople were usually freemen and freewomen. They paid rent to the lord for a house and garden. Craftspeople usually only worked in the fields at harvest, when everyone had to take part.

Alf Miller

"I run the mill and grind grain into flour for bread. I keep some of the finished flour as my payment. Some of what I earn goes to the lord as rent for the mill."

Widow Baker

"My family bakes the bread for everyone in the village oven. People usually pay us 'in kind.' That means we get paid in bread or other products such as eggs or vegetables. I'm training my son to take over as baker after me."

Robin Fuller

"I run the fulling mill. Weavers bring new woolen cloth to us. We clean it and pound it to tighten up the threads. This makes it warmer and more weatherproof."

Will Smith

"I can make and repair anything made of metal! Bring me your cart wheel rims, plough shares, knives, scythes for cutting grain, and scissors.

"I can make locks, keys, chains, and bolts, too. I have a boy who keeps the fire in the forge burning. He's going to have to get a lot stronger if he wants to be a blacksmith!"

Thomas Joiner

"A joiner is a wood worker. I make and repair stools, carts, and other wooden products.

"Sometimes I work with Adam Carpenter and Edgar Thatcher on houses. They build the structure and put on the thatched roof. I help them, but I mainly make furniture."

Legacy

Many common family names come from the craft or occupation of an ancestor (a member of the family from the past).

Do ◊ Discuss ◊ Discover

1. In groups of 3, choose three types of work described on pages 21–26. Discuss the importance of work done by both women and men.

2. As a class, list family names that may have come from past occupations.

Managers and Leaders

Villages and farms were managed by the lord's officials. They represented the lord, so others had to obey and respect them.

Steward

The **steward** acted as the business manager of the manor. Some lords had many pieces of land. The steward travelled from village to village and reported back to the lord. He kept the business records. Manors owned by abbeys always had stewards to manage the lands. The steward was an important person in the community.

Bailiff

The **bailiff** supervised jobs given to serfs. He oversaw the running of the village and enforced the lord's laws. If skilled craftspeople were needed, the bailiff hired them. When the village produced more crops than they needed, he sold the extra products. He also bought things the manor needed that were not produced there.

Reeve

The **reeve** could be either a serf or a freeman. He lived in the village and acted as a foreman of the other serfs. The reeve was chosen by other villagers. He organized village work such as planting and harvesting.

Tally Sticks

Stewards, bailiffs, and reeves needed to learn to keep accounts. The reeve often used a tally stick as a counting device. This helped him to keep accurate records of how much tax was paid and by whom. The steward and the lord carefully checked these records.

Legacy

The elected leader of the Council in some towns and rural districts is still called a reeve today.

The Village of Elton

The village of Elton in Cambridgeshire, England, was in a manor that belonged to the abbot of Abbey Ramsey. The abbot did not live in Elton and he rarely visited it. He had 23 other manors. The abbot's officials ran them and kept accounts recording the money spent and received.

In Elton, the Abbot of Ramsey had about [3 square kilometres] of land. There are now 4 ploughs on the [lord's portion of land]. There are 28 [serfs] who have 20 ploughs. There is a church and a priest, and 2 mills with an income of 40 shillings a year. There are [69 hectares] of meadow.

from the Domesday Book

The Domesday Book

The first record of Elton is in the Domesday Book. In the 1080s, the officials of King William I of England went all over England taking a census. They recorded everything that everyone owned in a huge book. The king used the information to set the taxes of all the people he ruled.

2 water mills and a fulling mill also belonged to the Abbot, also fishing rights on the river

from another royal survey 100 years later

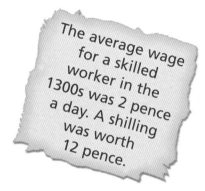

The average wage for a skilled worker in the 1300s was 2 pence a day. A shilling was worth 12 pence.

1 carpenter for 12 days
(for work on chapel) . . . . 12 pence

1 thatcher for 32 days, with food and lodging
(for thatching barn) . . . . 2 shillings

1 bolt (for door of little barn) . . . . . . 1 penny

1 carpenter for 6 days
(making gates for hall and barn) . . 6 pence

4 men for 3 weeks
(slating chapel roof) . . . 5 shillings 2 pence

2 carpenters for 3 1/2 days
(repairing building between mills) 7 pence

1 thatcher (thatching two mills) . . . 7 pence

from records of money spent by the lord in the 1300s

This replica of a thatched house in Sussex, England, has walls made of flint stones.

The Pin

Young Edgar's blind grandfather was sitting on a bench beside the wall braiding strips of hide into a rope. It was Michaelmas. The sun was still warm on this golden harvest day in September. Grandfather stopped Edgar as he trudged past. Edgar was exhausted from a long day of work, and hungry, as always.

"Come here, lad," Edgar's grandfather said. "It's time to show you who you really are."

Edgar's eyes opened wide. He was already ten years old and worked full time on the family's land. Next year, perhaps, he would guide the oxen as they plowed their deep furrows, or sow the seeds. His grandfather could no longer help with the heavy work, and the other children were still too young.

His family had worked on Sir Neville's land and lived in this house forever, he thought. He understood the family's duties and debts to the manor. They bowed their heads when the lords rode by. What more was there to know about who they were? He looked at his grandfather. "Who am I, then?" he asked.

Edgar's grandfather pulled a small leather pouch on a thong from under his tunic and carefully placed it on his knee. His fingers were twisted from old injuries and they trembled with pain. He slowly opened the pouch. A round gold object shone in the sun. Red and purple stones around its edges glowed as if filled with light.

Edgar froze with terror. Perhaps it was stolen! If the bailiff found out, they would all be hanged!

"This is a lord's sign, my boy," said Grandfather. Edgar saw tears in his grandfather's cloudy eyes. "It belonged to my grandfather. We were lords in this land long before the armies from Normandy came when I was a child. Always remember that we carry the blood of lords. When this is yours, you must protect it and be proud."

Suddenly Edgar understood why other people stepped to one side as his grandfather passed through the village. He had seen them nod respectfully. Edgar's heart beat faster. He would not forget.

Religion

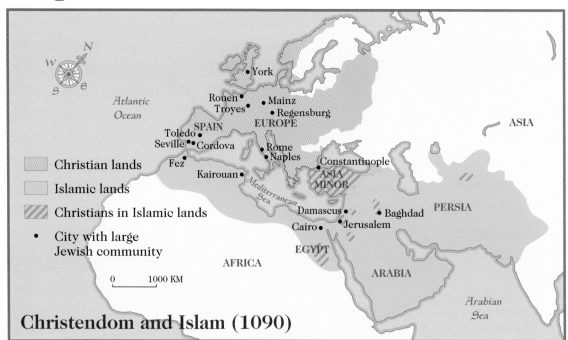

Christendom and Islam (1090)

Map legend:
- Christian lands
- Islamic lands
- Christians in Islamic lands
- • City with large Jewish community

0   1000 KM

Map labels: York, Rouen, Troyes, Mainz, Regensburg, Toledo, SPAIN, Seville, Cordova, Fez, Kairouan, EUROPE, Rome, Naples, Constantinople, ASIA MINOR, Damascus, Baghdad, PERSIA, Cairo, Jerusalem, EGYPT, ARABIA, AFRICA, ASIA, Atlantic Ocean, Mediterranean Sea, Arabian Sea

In medieval times, religion had an important place in everyday life. In England and much of Europe, most people were Christians. The area where Christians were in the majority was often called Christendom.

Followers of the Islamic religion, called Muslims, were rare in the north of Europe. They were in the majority in southern Spain, Persia, Asia Minor, Arabia, Egypt, and northern Africa. The name for this region was Islam. (You will find out more about Islam in Chapter 9.)

There were small numbers of Jewish people. They could only live in towns and cities and their lives were quite restricted.

Hinduism and Buddhism were important religions in Asia at this time.

Christianity

Christians believed that after death they would be punished for wrong-doings in life. They tried to earn rewards and avoid punishments in the afterlife. They attended church services, gave money to the Church and to the poor, and visited holy places called **shrines** to pray.

Latin

The language used in the Roman Catholic Church was Latin. Church services were said and sung in Latin. Clergy (priests and bishops) and members of religious communities (monks and nuns) learned to read and speak Latin. They could travel between religious centres and work wherever needed.

Ora et labora.
Pray and work.
–St. Benedict

The Village Priest

Every village had a priest. He held church services, prayed for sick people, and performed burials and baptisms. The priest heard people's confessions of wrong-doings. He gave them **penances** to perform to show they were sorry for their sins.

Village families brought their children to the priest to be baptised.

Priests received **tithes** on behalf of the Church. Tithes were a percentage of the villagers' goods (usually one-tenth). The Church taught people that it was their duty to support its work.

The priest was an important person in the village. He was granted a house and a small piece of land by the lord of the manor. He farmed the land to provide his food and income.

Village Education

The priest was usually the only person in the village who could teach children to read or write.

A well-off village freeman might pay for a son to be educated. Girls did not go to school. A freeman might also pay a monastery or convent to accept a son or daughter as a novice (beginner) monk or nun. Some paid the Church to train a son as a priest. Serfs did not have these opportunities.

Most children were taught by their parents to eventually take over their roles. Boys learned farm work or the father's craft. Girls learned their mother's skills.

A carpenter's son learned his father's craft by first making simple objects.

Holy Days and Festivals

Most manors had at least 15 holy days in a year. On those days, serfs did not work in the fields. Essential work such as milking was done. There were many different special saints' days. They were not all celebrated everywhere. However, the Christmas and Easter holy days were celebrated by all Christians.

On holy days, everyone went to church. Then they might go to a religious event such as a play based on a Bible story. Sometimes the churchyard was used as a meeting place. Tables were set up for eating and drinking.

Major festivals usually included a feast and dancing, music, and other types of entertainment. Tumblers and jugglers were popular. The lord of the manor often provided the food for the feast. Winter festivals often took place in the great hall of the manor house.

A Village Market

Villagers had few chances to travel or learn about the outside world. Travelling traders who visited villages were a source of news. They also carried items like salt, metal tools, needles, or coloured cloth. They traded goods to villagers for money or products like grain, flour, wool, or food. On the weekly market day, a large village bustled with activity.

Village Justice

The lord of the manor made the laws for the people who lived on it. The steward, bailiff, and reeve enforced the laws. The lord heard complaints, made decisions about quarrels, and set punishments for law-breaking.

The **manorial court** was usually held in the great hall of the manor house. Sometimes the steward acted as judge in the lord's place if the lord was absent. Serfs could not testify in the court. However, the reeve or bailiff could tell their stories.

There were few jails in medieval times. Justice for serious crimes was immediate, harsh, and usually related to the original crime. A thief caught stealing more than once might have a hand cut off. Serious offenders could be hanged or beheaded.

Minor offences often resulted in fines, which were paid to the lord. Wrongdoers might be placed in **stocks** in the common area. That meant they were locked in a wooden frame. Other people could ridicule and criticize them and throw rotten food at them.

Many laws that are used in Canada today came from English Common Law. Common law rules were agreed upon by most people. Everyone was expected to follow them.

Common law rules were sometimes used by courts to make decisions. These decisions were written down. Later, these legal decisions were referred to in other law cases.

The Supreme Court of Canada is Canada's highest court.

Asking Questions

Asking questions can help you learn more about people, history, and situations. Some types of questions are answered with a lot of information and explanation. Some are answered with a few particular facts. Both types are helpful. It depends on what information you are looking for.

Fact Questions

Fact questions usually have short answers that give limited, but specific, information. They often begin with words like

- Who
- What
- List
- Where
- When

Inquiry Questions

Inquiry (or "Why") questions ask for thoughtful answers that go beyond yes, no, or a simple fact. They provide expanded information and help you make sense of it. They often begin with words like

- Explain
- How
- Compare
- Give an example
- Describe
- Would
- Why

When preparing questions, think about the kinds of answers you need. Do you need simple facts, or explanations and descriptions?

Do ◊ Discuss ◊ Discover

1. Play the 10-question game. Form small groups of 3 or 4.

   a) One member of the group chooses a role of a person in a medieval village. This group member must be prepared to answer questions about the role using information from Chapters 1 and 2.

   b) The other group members work together to develop 10 questions to ask in order to learn the identity of the person in role.

Using Your Learning

Understanding Concepts

1. Using information from the Introduction and Chapters 1 and 2, explain in your notes the main differences between serfs and freemen/freewomen.

2. Make a web in your notes like the one shown below. Complete the web to show how religion was an important part of village life. Add more parts to the web as needed.

3. Identify vocabulary from Chapter 2 to add to the Vocabulary section of your notebook. Add diagrams or sketches to help you remember the words and their meanings.

Developing Inquiry/Research and Communication Skills

4. Use library resources (or visit http://scholar.chem.nyu.edu/technology.html) to find information on medieval farming technology. Write 5–6 sentences about your findings. Include diagrams if available.

Applying Skills and Concepts in Various Contexts

5. Create a word collage on a blank sheet of 28 cm x 43 cm (11" x 17") paper. Think of words that describe medieval village life. Write these words all over the paper. Use colour, interesting lettering, and/or illustrations. Share your word collage with another student.

6. Imagine you are a boy or girl living in a medieval village. Write a diary entry describing a typical day.

Medieval Times Project

1. As a group, list the different types of games you have researched. Discuss the advantages and disadvantages of each type of game. Will it be fun to play? Will it be easy or difficult to build? Will it help the players learn about medieval times?

2. Choose a type of game to design. You can use a combination of ideas from two or more games.

3. Review Chapter 2. Identify key information about village life that you wish to include in your game. Then write questions and answers. Keep these in your folder to work on later.

Chapter 3
A Medieval Castle

Kings and powerful nobles built castles for protection and to show their power. They lived in their castles some of the time and in manor houses on their lands at other times. Less powerful nobles often did not own castles. They received protection in return for providing fighting men and support.

Focus on Learning

In this chapter you will learn about
- changes in castle design
- building a castle
- constructing models
- inside a castle
- parts of a castle

Vocabulary

motte and bailey	solar
keep	garderobe
curtain wall	moat
seige	drawbridge
stonemason	portcullis

Castle Design

Castles were built on a site that was easy to defend, such as a high cliff. Castle design changed as weapons and methods of warfare changed.

About 1000...

- A wooden tower surrounded by a protective wall was built on a mound of earth (**motte**).
- A fenced area (**bailey**) at the bottom of the hill protected local people in time of war.

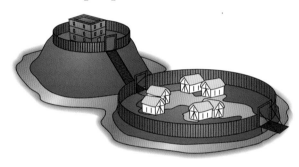

Before stone castles were common, wooden motte and bailey castles were used for defence.

About 1170...

- The lord's family lived in the stone **keep** (tower).
- Stone **curtain walls** surrounded the entire castle complex.
- Towers were added along the curtain wall for defence.
- Houses, kitchens, wells, stables, and other buildings were built inside the curtain wall.
- A castle needed to be self-sufficient when under **siege** (when attackers surrounded it and prevented supplies of food and water from reaching it).

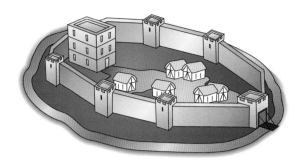

Stone walls did not burn when fire-throwing weapons were used. War machines were used to batter walls with stones.

About 1300...

- Castles had much larger, thicker walls, with round towers.
- The lord's home was larger and more comfortable.

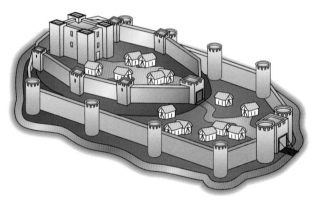

Digging under the wall weakened it so attackers could break in. Round towers were more difficult for enemies to undermine.

About 1400...

Cannons were developed that could batter down most stone walls. After that, warfare changed. Battles on open fields away from castles were more usual.

Most nobles returned to living in their manor houses. Only kings and a few nobles still lived in castles.

Building a Castle

A large stone castle was expensive to build. It might take ten or more years to complete. Many men, animals, and machines were needed to do the work. Serfs from the manor had to spend some time working on the castle. That left fewer men to work in the fields. Serfs cleared land, cut stone blocks, cut trees, and did rough building work. Craftspeople were paid, but serfs usually were not.

Deep foundations were needed to support the weight of the castle. Foundation trenches were filled with rocks or dug down to bedrock. The double outer wall was up to six metres thick at the base. It was filled with rocks and rubble.

Carpenters built wooden platforms and scaffolding. They added wooden floors and roof beams when the stone work was done.

1 Materials were carried or dragged up wooden ramps and along platforms.

2 Cranes, pulleys, and winches were used to raise stone and other materials.

3 Mortar to cement the stones together was a mixture of sand, lime, and water.

4 To raise the heaviest blocks of stone, one to three people walked inside a treadmill. The large wheel was connected to a pulley system on a crane.

Stonemasons

Master **stonemasons** had the skills of architects and engineers. They designed, planned, and supervised the building of huge stone structures. Medieval castles and cathedrals were built by stonemasons.

Masons went through different stages of training until they were qualified. They had different types of skills. Some masons worked mainly on building. Some specialized in carving figures, stone decorations, and columns to support roofs.

Cranes, pulleys, winches, ropes, chains, ramps, and human and animal strength were used to lift and move building materials. No power tools were available. Stone was cut and shaped by hand. Tools were similar to hand tools used today.

The master mason planned and supervised the job. He created the design.

Free masons were fully trained and could take contracts under different masters.

Rough masons cut and shaped the rough stone blocks.

Elsewhere...

Himeji Castle in Japan was built of stone and wood. Its huge size showed the power of the warlord and his warriors, who were called *samurai*.

Legacy

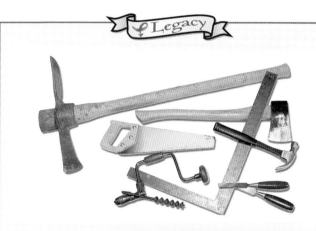

These tools are still used in the same ways as medieval builders used them.

Do ◊ Discuss ◊ Discover

1. Draw and label tools on pages 38 and 39 that look familiar to you. Describe their uses to a classmate.

Constructing Models

A model is a small form of something larger. Models show details of important parts of the original, but they are also simplified. For example, the wheels of a model car turn, but the motor usually doesn't run.

Making a Three-dimensional Model

1. Analyse the features of the original object. Use photographs or diagrams if you cannot view the object itself.

   • What features are the most important and must be shown?

   • What features can be shown by drawing on the surface or left out?

   • Will the model need to have moving parts?

2. Decide what size the model will be, compared to the original. This is the scale. For example, the model of a 10 m by 20 m house could be 10 cm by 20 cm. All of the parts of a model should be in the same scale (for example, the windows, doors, walls, roof).

3. Decide what materials to use to represent the original (for example, paper, cardboard, plastic, wood, string). How will you fasten them together (for example, glue, tape)?

4. Decide how to add details and represent the materials, colours, textures, and patterns of the original (for example, glue on sand, string, or pieces of cardboard; add paint; cut holes).

5. Plan your construction. Measure and cut out the pieces.

6. Experiment with difficult parts. For example, how will moving parts be held in place? How will the frame be braced so it does not collapse? Make any necessary changes to your plan.

7. Tape the parts together with masking tape first, before gluing, to make sure your plan will work. Decorate or add details to pieces before they are glued into place.

8. Place the finished model on a base so it can be moved safely, displayed, and stored.

Making a Builder's Crane

You will need

- cardboard
- 50 cm string
- 10–12 wooden craft sticks
- 1 bamboo skewer
- two small pulleys
- white glue, tape
- scissors
- pencil, ruler

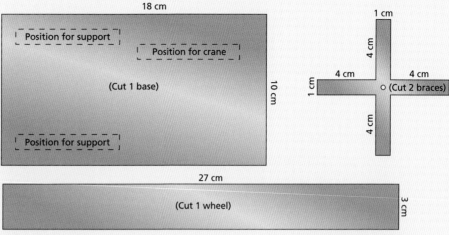

18 cm

Position for support

Position for crane

(Cut 1 base)

10 cm

1 cm

4 cm

1 cm | 4 cm | 4 cm

○ (Cut 2 braces)

4 cm

Position for support

27 cm

(Cut 1 wheel)

3 cm

1. Measure, draw, and cut out from cardboard the treadmill wheel, braces, and base shown above.

2. Draw or paint steps onto the wheel strip. Roll the strip into a circle and tape it firmly. Make a hole at the centre point of each brace. Assemble and glue the treadmill wheel as shown in **A**.

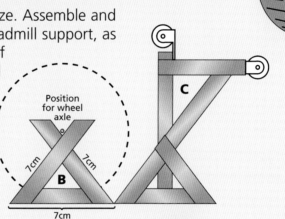

3. Cut wooden craft sticks to size. Assemble and glue the two sides of the treadmill support, as shown in **B**. Glue the sides of the support to the cardboard base 6 cm apart. Cut a 9 cm-piece of bamboo skewer. Place it through the holes in the braces as an axle. Place the axle ends on the supports.

Position for wheel axle

7cm 7cm

B

7cm

C

4. Assemble and glue the crane shown in **C**. Glue the bottom to the cardboard base.

5. Attach one pulley to each end of the crane. (Methods will vary for different types of pulleys.) Glue one end of the string to the axle beside the treadmill wheel. Then wind half of the string onto it. Feed the string over the two crane pulleys and down to attach it to the load.

41

Inside a Castle

The earliest castles were not very comfortable. They were built as a fort, to defend the noble family. Knights and soldiers stayed in them when needed. There was little furniture and rooms were often cold. However, by about 1200, the lord and lady had well-furnished rooms. There were huge fireplaces for warmth and candles for light.

The lord and lady's private rooms might be in the keep or elsewhere in the castle. The illustration on this page shows the family's rooms in a tower.

The **solar** was a private area for the lord's family and personal servants. Women sewed, played music, or painted, and children played quiet games. The lord might read documents of the manor or receive a guest for a private visit.

1 the lady's wardrobe, used to store clothing and bedding

2 the lord and lady's bedchamber

3 the solar

4 the basement, used to store valuables

Wooden floors of castles were often covered with mats made of the long, flat leaves of rushes. Wealthy lords used carpets in private rooms in later medieval times.

Rooms were furnished with stools, benches, and chests to store clothes, bedding, and valuables.

Fireplaces were built into the walls. Smoke was carried away between the walls.

Castle windows were small and the walls very thick. Candles made of wax or tallow (animal fat) were used for light.

Beds had leather thongs laced across the frame to support a mattress stuffed with feathers. Bed curtains provided some privacy and extra warmth. Children or a servant might sleep in a pull-out bed below.

Walls were plastered and whitewashed with lime. Some might be painted with patterns or murals. Cloth hangings on the walls helped keep out drafts and added colour to rooms.

Toilets called **garderobes** were built into the walls of the castle. A bench with a hole cut in it was suspended over the moat or a cesspit below. From time to time, a servant had the job of cleaning out the pit.

The lowest floor of a castle keep usually contained storage areas. It might also have a dungeon where prisoners were kept.

The lord of the manor entertained guests and held public activities in the great hall of the castle. The lord and lady and special guests sat on a raised platform at one end of the hall.

The lord, his family, and the knights spent part of their day praying in the castle chapel.

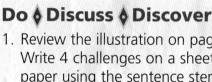

Do ◊ Discuss ◊ Discover

1. Review the illustration on page 42. Write 4 challenges on a sheet of paper using the sentence stem "Find the …." Trade lists with a partner. See who can find all four challenges first.

Parts of a Castle

Castles needed many facilities to make them self-sufficient.

1 The **moat** was filled with water after the castle was finished.

2 The **drawbridge** over the moat could be raised and lowered.

3 A strong gate called a **portcullis** could be raised high in the arch above the castle entrance or lowered to bar the way.

4 A gatehouse guarded the castle entrance.

5 The curtain wall enclosed the entire castle complex.

6 Spiral staircases in the towers connected several storeys.

7 Stables housed the war horses and the horses for hunting and riding.

8 Armour and weapons for the lord and his knights were made and repaired in the armoury.

Bodiam Castle was built in the 1300s.

9 In some castles, the lord and lady's private bedchamber, solar, and **10** garden were separate from the keep.

11 Most castles had a chapel.

12 The keep contained a great hall where the knights met for meals. In many castles, the family's rooms were on the top floors of the keep.

13 A covered well supplied water to the castle.

14 The kitchen might be attached to the castle or in a separate building because of the threat of fire. The oven might be separate or in the kitchen.

15 Herb and vegetable gardens provided food and healing herbs.

16 In some castles, a windmill for grinding grain stood where it caught the wind. Earlier castles used water mills.

17 Castle craftspeople, servants, and some serfs who looked after fields and animals had homes inside the walls.

18 The bailey was an open area. Buildings ringed the inner walls.

Using Your Learning

Understanding Concepts

1. Review this chapter. Identify and explain the different things in a castle design that were meant to protect the people inside. Put the information in a chart in your notebook.

2. Compare a room in a castle with a room in a village house (page 10). List one similarity and two differences.

3. Identify vocabulary from Chapter 3 to add to the Vocabulary section of your notebook. Add diagrams or sketches to help you remember the words and their meanings.

Developing Inquiry/Research and Communication Skills

4. Do research on an existing castle using the library and Internet. List in your notes five facts that you find.

5. Creat a diorama of *one room* of a castle.

6. Design a piece of furniture for a castle. Construct a model of your design. Refer to page 40 for information about constructing models.

Applying Skills and Concepts in Various Contexts

7. Use a graphic organizer to compare technology used to build castles with technology used to build large structures in Canada today.

8. Discuss with a partner features of modern buildings that provide protection against break-ins.

Medieval Times Project

1. As a group, review your decision about the type of board game you wish to design. Discuss any changes you want to make to the idea.

2. Make a checklist of tasks that need to be done for your project.

3. Decide what elements your game will include besides a game board. Some examples are game pieces, cards, dice, score cards, and instructions. Make notes about your group's decisions and put them into your folder.

4. Identify key information about medieval castles from Chapter 3 and write questions and answers. Keep them in your folder to work on later.

Chapter 4

Castle Life

People from all levels of medieval society lived in a castle. These usually included a lord, his lady, knights, **ladies-in-waiting** who serve the lady, **squires** training to be knights, craftspeople, servants of all kinds, a priest, serfs, and labourers. Work, education, and entertainment often went on at the same time.

Focus on Learning

In this chapter you will learn about
- the people who lived in a castle
- the food and clothing of lords and ladies
- learning through comparing
- the role of the lord of the manor
- the lady of the manor and children
- workers in the castle
- knighthood
- castle entertainment
- religious life and education

Vocabulary

lady-in-waiting	chain mail
squire	heraldry
page	pilgrim
trencher	relic
alms	ransom
chivalry	

A Castle Community

The earliest castles were forts built for times of war. Knights and soldiers came to the castle for training. They defended it whenever they were needed. It was too expensive to pay and feed them full time.

The lord and his family lived in the castle when it was in use. The rest of the time they lived in their manor houses.

Boys and young men from noble families usually went to live in another family's castle. They received part of their education and training there. A **page** was a young boy who served and did errands for the lord or lady. Often, a page later became a squire and trained to be a knight.

In the castles of the highest nobles, the lady was attended by girls from other noble houses. These were her ladies-in-waiting. They acted as her companions and helped her with her work.

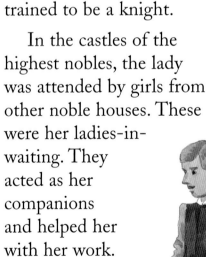

The lord's trusted officials like the steward also came from noble families. Connections between families were important.

Large castles employed as many as one hundred servants. They had all kinds of duties. Most of the servants were men or boys. In some castles, only the laundry workers and the lady's servants were female.

Castles had to be self-sufficient. Castle craftspeople built, made, and repaired almost everything needed in daily life. Serfs handled the animals, worked in the kitchens, and did manual labour.

Food

Cooks, bakers, butchers, and ale-makers made food for the castle community. Kitchen servants prepared and served it.

Bread was a staple. Nobles liked white bread. Darker, heavier bread was made for servants and fighting men. Old bread was soaked in wine, ale, or milk for breakfast.

People in castles ate many of the same grain, vegetable, and dairy foods eaten in the village. Pigs and chickens were also raised as food. Hunters provided extra meat from wild birds and animals for banquets.

The nobles liked interesting flavours from spices, sweets, and rich sauces for their meats. Spices were expensive luxuries. They were used in food served to important guests.

Spices
pepper
cinnamon
cloves
ginger
nutmeg
saffron

Serving Food

The main meal was eaten at midday. Trumpets announced the meal, and everyone ate together in the great hall.

Meat pies were often baked in decorated pie crusts. Whole birds or animals were cooked and decorated. Then they were presented with ceremony at the lord's table.

Food was served in bowls shared between people. Most people ate their food from a **trencher**, which was a thick piece of old bread. These gravy-soaked trenchers were often given to poor people after the meal.

Everyone carried a knife for cutting up pieces of food. Spoons for serving food were provided, but there were no forks. People ate with their fingers. Bones were put into a bowl or tossed to the floor for the dogs.

Salt was used for preserving food, and it once was more valuable than gold. The ship on this table contained salt. Salt was used only on the lord's table, which was "above the salt." Less important people sat "below the salt."

Clothing

In early medieval times, the lady and the other women sewed all of the family's clothing. They added embroidery for decoration.

In later medieval times, styles were elaborate. People used their clothing to show how wealthy they were. Rich types of cloth such as silk were imported from other countries. Some merchants brought cloth to the castle and displayed it for the lord and lady. Otherwise, cloth was bought at a fair. Tailors were often paid to sew clothing.

A squire had the job of helping the lord dress in his layers of clothing. A lady-in-waiting helped the lady.

The length of a man's shirt and surcoat was a sign of wealth. Long robes showed a man could afford as much cloth as he wanted. It showed he did not have to work.

Wooden platforms were tied on to protect shoes from mud and dirt.

❶ The lord's ankle-length shirt had long tight sleeves. Buttons were invented in the 1200s.

❷ A surcoat (over-garment) was worn with a belt. The neck was often fastened by a brooch or pin.

❸ The lord's woolen stockings were held up with ties called points. A loose pair of underpants was fastened with a cloth belt.

❹ Money was carried in a small purse hung from the belt.

❺ Rings and other jewellery showed wealth and importance.

❶ The lady wore a linen underdress that hung to her feet.

❷ She wore a sleeveless surcoat over a long-sleeved dress.

❸ A headdress with a veil covered her hair. This showed she was married—unmarried girls often wore their hair down.

Comparison

When you compare things, you think about ways they are similar and different. You can compare any two things that have some qualities in common. Comparing similarities and differences can help you come to a conclusion, form an opinion, or see things in a new way.

One way to show comparison is to use an organizer. One type of organizer is shown below.

1. Identify what you are comparing and label the two sides, **A** and **B**.

2. In the centre space, list the criteria or items you are comparing.

3. Fill in information for both sides.

4. Review the information to find similarities and differences.

5. Develop conclusions based on your review.

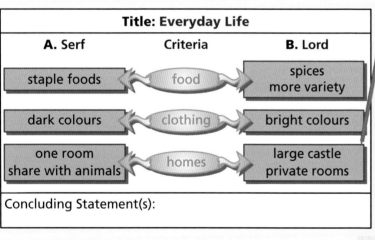

Title: Everyday Life		
A. Serf	**Criteria**	**B. Lord**
staple foods	food	spices more variety
dark colours	clothing	bright colours
one room share with animals	homes	large castle private rooms

Concluding Statement(s):

Do ◆ Discuss ◆ Discover

1. Make a comparison organizer in your notebook. Compare *Life in a Medieval Castle* with *Life in a Modern Home*. Think of at least 4 criteria to compare. Complete your organizer. Remember to write a conclusion telling which you think would be better and why.

2. Write two concluding statements in your notebook for the example on this page.

The Lord

The lord's role was to support the king, make decisions for the manor and his family, and act as a leader.

A lord was expected to prepare for and fight in wars and attend the king's court. Often he rode around his lands to inspect work and make decisions. When he was in the castle or manor house, he held court in the great hall.

In his court, the lord gave judgements on serious crimes and minor broken rules. There were many household rules. Stealing, swearing, drunkenness, and fighting might be punished by a fine or time in the stocks. The lord could order a public whipping for more serious crimes. Punishments for the most serious crimes were severe.

The lord toured the armouries and stables and watched knights and squires practise swordplay. If he could read, he reviewed documents and accounts. Stewards, bailiffs, and senior castle servants often gave spoken reports. They suggested purchases or changes needed, and he made decisions.

Guests and travellers often stayed at castles. If guests were of noble birth, the lord entertained them at the high table. Other visitors were placed with those of a similar social group.

The lord and his family went to the chapel for prayer. He also gave **alms** to the poor. Alms might be given as money, food, clothing, or shoes.

The Lady

The lady's role was to manage the castle community of family and servants. She was also in charge when the lord went to war. If the castle was attacked, she might direct the defence. However, the lady's duties were usually more peaceful.

Role of a Lady
- obey the lord's wishes
- supervise the children and women
- order supplies to be purchased
- manage the work of the servants
- supervise all cloth and clothing making: carding (combing) wool, spinning, weaving, dyeing, sewing, and embroidering
- entertain visitors

Children

A number of servants helped the lady raise and care for her children. Fathers were usually in charge of discipline, which was sometimes harsh.

Children of noble families were sometimes taught to read and write and do arithmetic. Girls learned to sing, play musical instruments, and dance. Children's toys included toy soldiers, hobby-horses, and dolls.

Children learned the roles they would have as adults. Most boys and some girls went to live with a noble neighbour or relative at about the age of seven. Boys were pages. Girls were ladies-in-waiting and learned how to run a household.

Most girls married between the ages of 12 and 14. Girls' parents arranged marriages to suitable young men. Marriages were important connections between noble families. Some girls were given permission to become a nun instead of marrying. Occasionally, boys became monks or priests if they did not become knights.

Do ◊ Discuss ◊ Discover

1. Draw a chart to list the duties of the lord, lady, and children. Fill it in and put it into your notebook.

Workers in the Castle

There were many craftspeople, servants, and other workers in the castle. There was a baker, butcher, and miller. Carpenters, joiners, and stonemasons did building and repairs. These are some others:

The Steward
"I act as business manager and look after the lord's finances and supplies."

The Priest
"I lead services in the chapel, act as secretary, and tutor the children. I also help write legal documents and letters."

The Marshal
"I supervise and train the knights' horses. The lord trusts me to help make decisions in the castle."

The Armourer
"My workers and I provide the lord's most important technology. We make and repair weapons, armour, locks, keys, and other metal objects in the castle armoury."

The Falconer
"I keep and train the falcons and hawks. The lord and lady use them for hunting."

The Huntsman
"I train and look after the hunting dogs and the horses used for hunting."

The Pantler
"I look after the food supplies for the castle."

The Butler
"I look after the castle's supplies of wine."

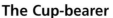

The Cup-bearer
"I stand at the lord's elbow and pour his wine during meals."

The Ewerer
"I am responsible for the lord and lady's table linen. It's valuable and needs careful cleaning."

A Groom
"We feed and look after all the horses, from the great warhorses to the young master's pony."

Do ◆ Discuss ◆ Discover

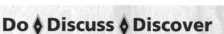

1. As a class, discuss reasons why there were so many different workers in a castle.
2. Write a short paragraph explaining which job you think is the most interesting, and why.

A Squire's Last Day

Phillip and John are cousins living in Banbury Castle. Phillip is to be knighted the next day. John, who is still a page, helps him prepare.

John: I'm sorry. I didn't mean to pull your hair. I'm just nervous.

Phillip: I should not be so impatient. I'm nervous, too. I'll need the cloak, John. It will be cold in the chapel.

John: It is cold everywhere. Why did you have to bathe, anyway?

Phillip: It's a symbol. The bath water is meant to wash away all my bad habits and nasty thoughts. I will also spend tonight alone in the chapel praying. I must enter into the state of knighthood with a pure mind and a clean body. The oath will be sworn before God.

John: Yes, but you had to satisfy Sir Godfrey first to become a knight. You have been his squire for four years, and a page in this castle before that. Did you always know you would become a knight?

Phillip: I always wanted to be a knight, and Father expects it. He sent me to serve in Sir Godfrey's household so I would be trained well. I have had wonderful experiences. I have attended many tournaments. I also accompanied him to France on a secret mission for the king. Of course, I can't tell you about that, on my honour.

John: I wish I could do something like that. Maybe, some day… Anyway, here is your sword belt, but no sword. Tomorrow, Sir Godfrey will touch your shoulder with the flat of his sword and dub you, Sir Knight. Then you will get your own sword and spurs.

Phillip: Yes, Father had a new sword made for me. It is engraved, and our family motto is inlaid in silver. I am honoured. I am also grateful that Father can afford to give me the equipment that I need. A knight is not very well paid, you know!

John: But you may earn more at tournaments! Someday you may fight in a war and take a noble prisoner, and a huge price will be paid for his return!

Phillip (laughing): Hold fast, young rooster. First I must become a knight, and before that I must go to the chapel, so I will bid you good night.

John: And also to you, Phillip.

Knights

A knight was a warrior who fought on horseback. He promised loyalty and service to his lord and to the king.

Medieval poetry and songs tell about knights that were brave, daring, loyal, wise, handsome, and had perfect manners. They protected women and were sincere Christians. This was called **chivalry**. Young men tried to be like the ideal, but war was harsh and violent.

The technology that a knight used for fighting slowly changed during the medieval period. Most knights wore chain mail for protection.

The Knight's Warhorse

Warhorses had to be strong to carry a knight wearing armour. They were trained to withstand battle conditions. Warhorses were expensive. They could cost a knight more than one year's income. He also needed horses for riding and hunting and a pack horse to carry armour and supplies. The warhorse was used only in battle or for tournaments.

Chain mail was made from row after row of interlocking steel rings. A padded under-tunic prevented the rings from cutting into the flesh. Mail shirts weighed between 9 and 27 kilograms.

Plate armour was more common after 1400. A suit made of curved metal plates was made to fit the knight exactly. The pieces were tied with leather thongs onto a padded undergarment.

Elsewhere...

Aztec warriors in what is now Mexico fought with spears and small shields. They wore a costume of an animal or bird to show they got their strength or skill from it.

Tournaments

Tournaments were organized competitions. They gave knights practice in the skills of combat. Knights were supposed to capture, not kill each other. They could become known for their bravery and strength.

The winners received money, horses, or other valuables from the losers' families or manors. Some knights made good livings at tournaments, like professional athletes today.

Originally, tournaments were like mass battles. The knights all charged each other. Many were killed or seriously wounded. Later, the Church and nobles made rules so tournaments would be safer.

Lords and kings hosted tournaments and invited knights to them. They usually built a grandstand for the ladies and nobles to watch the games. Ladies often gave a token, such as a scarf, to a knight to wear for luck.

Jousting became more common in the late medieval period. In a joust, two knights charged each other on horseback. Each carried a wooden lance, shield, and sword. When one knight was knocked off his horse, the other dismounted. Then they fought with swords. When one was injured, the lord called a halt and named the winner.

As time went on, tournaments became more like festivals than contests in battle. Flags flew, people dressed in their best clothes, and everyone cheered for their favourite knights.

Heraldry

Heraldry was a system of symbols that gave information about a noble family. The types of lines, colours, patterns, and symbols used in coats of arms all had special names.

Children inherited their noble father's coat of arms. When a noble lady with no brothers married, her family's coat of arms was joined with her husband's. The children inherited a "quartered" coat of arms, like the example on this page, when their father died.

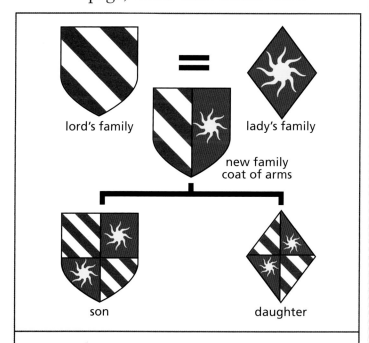

lord's family

lady's family

new family coat of arms

son

daughter

first son

second son

third son

While a noble man lived, his sons were identified with a symbol added to the family coat of arms.

Do ◊ Discuss ◊ Discover

1. Review pages 54–57 and make point-form notes of key information. Check your notes with a classmate.

Making a Shield

You will need
- bristol board (45 cm x 30 cm)
- strip of fabric (5 cm x 40 cm)
- acrylic paints
- ruler, scissors, glue

1. Research heraldry symbols. Decide what symbols to use and then sketch a design in your notebook.

2. Cut a shield shape (or diamond shape) from the bristol board. Draw, then paint, your design on one side of the bristol board.

3. Cut the fabric into two strips. Glue the ends of each strip to the back of the shield to form a loop. Leave room for your left arm to slide through the bottom loop so your hand can grasp the upper one. (If you made a diamond shape, make a loop to hang it for display.)

Entertainment

Work took up most of medieval people's time. However, sometimes there was time for games on holy days and festival days, after attending church services.

Types of chess, tic-tac-toe, backgammon, and checkers were some indoor games played in castles.

Minstrels and troubadours told stories and sang of heroes and kings.

Jesters sometimes performed comedy in nobles' great halls. Jesters could tell a joke at the lord's expense.

However, they had to be careful so they were not punished for their joke.

Tennis, croquet, and bowling are all games that were played in medieval times.

Few people read for entertainment. Books were rare and many people could not read. Storytelling was a favourite pastime. Travelling storytellers and singers were paid to entertain at banquets or in the lord and lady's private apartments.

The gittern was a popular musical instrument in medieval times.

Religious Life

In medieval times, the majority of people in Europe were Christians. The official church in western Europe was the Roman Catholic Church. The Church had many levels of powerful leaders, including the pope, cardinals, archbishops, bishops, and abbots. Nuns, monks, and village priests formed the largest group.

Both nuns and monks wore long robes tied with a rope belt. Nuns wore a headdress called a wimple that covered their hair and throat. Monks had part of their heads shaved to leave a circle of hair like a halo.

Pope

Cardinals & Archbishops

Bishops & Abbots

Nuns, Monks, & Priests

Both men and women could choose a religious life. They were expected to give up all of their goods and wealth to the Church and take a vow of poverty. They also promised not to marry and to always obey the rules of the Church. Monks and nuns lived in religious communities and spent their time in study, prayer, and work. Some religious communities ran schools and hospitals.

Bells rang to call monks and nuns for meals and prayers. Seven church services were sung or chanted during each day and night. Someone read aloud during meals while everyone else was silent.

Do ◆ Discuss ◆ Discover

1. Review page 6. Add the organization of the Church to one side of the pyramid you made on page 7.

Pilgrimages

Pilgrims were travellers who journeyed to visit shrines in holy places. Some people went on pilgrimages to give thanks to God. Others were seeking healing or a miracle. Many medieval people believed that pilgrimages would benefit them in the afterlife. They hoped to earn forgiveness for their sins.

This badge was worn by pilgrims who visited Saint Thomas à Becket's shrine in Canterbury.

Pilgrims often visited places where **relics** of saints were kept. Relics were religious objects such as a bone or a possession of a saint believed to have special powers. Medals or badges that could be attached to a hat or cloak were sold to pilgrims as souvenirs.

A relic of Saint Eustace was kept in this container.

Pilgrims of all different social groups often travelled together for protection. They were on a holy journey, so they did not carry weapons. Wealthy people often hired guards. Other travellers joined groups of pilgrims because it was safer than being alone on a journey.

Travellers had to be careful not to be robbed, killed, or kidnapped. The relatives of kidnapped people might be asked to pay a **ransom** for them to be freed. Sometimes, they would be sold as slaves.

The Canterbury Tales

Pilgrimages became so popular that the English writer Geoffrey Chaucer wrote a long poem called *The Canterbury Tales* about a group of pilgrims. The pilgrims were travelling to the cathedral in Canterbury, England, to visit the shrine of Saint Thomas à Becket.

Do ◆ Discuss ◆ Discover

1. As a class, discuss why it would have been important to a pilgrim to have a pilgrim's badge or to see a relic.

Using Your Learning

Understanding Concepts

1. Make a web in your notes like the one shown below. Complete the web to show how religion was an important part of castle life. Add more parts to the web as needed.

2. Identify vocabulary from Chapter 4 to add to the Vocabulary section of your notebook. Add diagrams or sketches to help you remember the words and their meanings.

Developing Inquiry/Research and Communication Skills

3. Use library resources (or visit www.dartfordarchive.org.uk/index.shtml) to find information on pilgrims. Research the clothing pilgrims wore. Draw a picture of a pilgrim and write a brief description for your notebook.

4. Design a poster to advertise a tournament. Since most people did not read in medieval times, use pictures and few words. Remember to add the time, date, and place it will be held.

Applying Skills and Concepts in Various Contexts

5. Choose *one* of the following topics:
   - tournaments today
   - home entertainment today

   Write three statements about the topic. Then write 2–3 sentences comparing the topic to medieval times.

Medieval Times Project

1. Review the goals of your game: to be fun to play and to help the players learn. Make final decisions about the type of board game and different elements the game will include.

2. On a large sheet of newsprint, begin to design the board. Some things to consider are ways of using the space, the start/end points, challenges/rewards for players, and illustrations to decorate your game board.

3. As you work on the board together, make notes about the instructions for playing the game. This is part of the game design.

4. Identify key information about castle life from Chapter 4 and write questions and answers. Keep them in your folder to work on later.

Chapter 5
Medieval Towns and Cities

Towns and cities are centres where many people live together and make their livings in different ways. Between 1100 and 1300, many medieval villages grew into towns with hundreds of houses, businesses, and large churches. Pollution and fires were problems when so many people lived close together.

Focus on Learning

In this chapter you will learn about
• the growth of towns
• town streets and homes
• note-making
• cathedrals
• a profile of a medieval town

Vocabulary

charter	Romanesque
town council	Gothic
curfew	buttress

The Growth of Towns

In early medieval times, wealthy nobles and the Church controlled most of the land. Most people lived in rural villages and worked on farms. In the 1100s, only 10% to 15% of the people in England lived in towns and cities.

By the 1200s, business and trade greatly increased. Wealth came to be measured in terms of money rather than land. Towns were an important part of this change.

Most townspeople were freemen and freewomen. Many produced products for sale. Others provided skills and services for money.

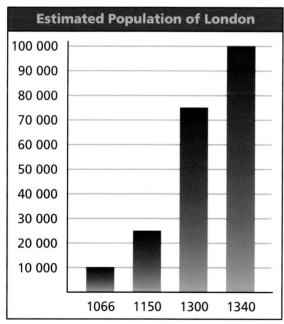

Estimated Population of London

London was a city. It grew rapidly during medieval times, until a disaster struck. You will read more about this in Chapter 10.

A Town Charter

Towns usually began as part of a lord's property. The lord had authority over town business. He received rents and taxes from the townspeople.

As townspeople became more wealthy, many wanted to govern themselves. People from some towns asked the king to approve a **charter** for them. They needed the king's seal on a document to make them independent from the local lord. They paid the king a sum of money for it.

Important townspeople established a **town council**. The council made many of the decisions for the townspeople. The lord still received some taxes. However, he had less say in the way the town was run.

This charter with King John's seal gave Londoners permission to elect their own mayor.

Do ◊ Discuss ◊ Discover

1. Look at the graph on this page. How much did the population of London grow between 1066 and 1340? Why do you think it grew so much?

2. Look at the three signs hanging over the shops on page 62. Predict with a partner what you think each shop sells and why they used symbols like these on their signs.

Town Streets

Towns and cities became smelly, crowded, and dirty as more people moved into them. They were usually built within walls for protection. Space was limited. Narrow, winding streets were crowded with animals, carts, and people.

Most streets were packed earth. They turned to mud when it rained. There were no sewers or garbage collection. An open ditch usually ran down the middle of the street. Garbage, washing water, and the contents of chamber pots were thrown into the ditch or onto the street. Many people owned chickens, goats, pigs, and other animals. Sometimes animals wandered around the streets.

The main roads entering the town came through large gates in the town wall. The gates were closed at night. The wall was used for defence against attack or robbers.

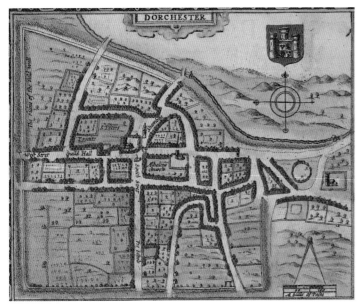

Although this plan of Dorchester, England, was made after the medieval period ended, it shows how the medieval town centre was laid out.

Streets were usually named after an important feature, like Bridge Street or Church Street. When several members of a craft had shops in the same area, the street might be named after them. For example, many tailors once lived on Threadneedle Street in London. The signs on people's shops showed a symbol of a product or a craft. For example, a loaf of bread marked a bakeshop and a pair of scissors marked a cloth seller.

Important public events happened in the town square. The square was located in front of the cathedral or the largest church, in the centre of the town. The weekly market would be held there.

Every town had at least one church, and often several. In 1340, the city of London had over 200 churches, and a population of 100 000.

The Night Watch

There were no street lights. Streets were patrolled by guards called the watch. The night watch carried lanterns on long poles through the dark narrow streets. They were responsible for enforcing the **curfew**. The word curfew came from the French phrase *couvrefeu*. It meant to cover your fire with a clay pot and go to bed. Fires were dangerous, so people had to put them out at night. After the curfew bell rang, the town gates were closed. No one could leave or enter the town until daybreak.

Elsewhere...

In the southwest of the United States, people built huge houses like apartment complexes out of stone. Cetro Ketl was built between 1020 and 1100 CE. It had about 500 rooms. A network of roads connected these houses to each other and to the extensive trading routes.

Do ◊ Discuss ◊ Discover

1. Identify possible causes of pollution in medieval towns and cities. Put these in your notebook under the title Causes of Pollution. Leave room to add to this list later.

Town Houses

Town houses were often several storeys tall. They were usually narrow across the front and built close beside each other. Home owners were taxed on their house's width along the street.

The family workshop or business was on the ground floor. The entrance to the living quarters was beside it.

The house's frame was constructed from wooden posts and beams.

The spaces between the wooden posts were filled with plaster.

In early medieval times, roofs were thatched. Slate or clay tiles became more common because fire was a threat in the crowded towns. Thatched roofs were too flammable.

The upper floors of town houses frequently jutted out over the street. This provided more living space. The solar (living room), kitchen, and bedrooms were often on the second floor. Large houses might have bedrooms on a third floor.

Sometimes the family had a garderobe, or toilet, that emptied into a pit in the basement or beside the house. Otherwise, the latrine (outhouse) was in the back yard.

Often several houses shared a well for their water supply.

Legacy

The width of a property along the street is called frontage. This is still a common basis for home and business taxes.

Note-making

Your notebook is a place to keep information about what you have been studying. Making notes will help you better understand the information you are learning. It will also help you remember. You can also use your notes to study for tests or prepare for projects.

One form of note-making is called T-Notes. T-Notes combine written notes and drawings.

Doing T-Notes

1. Write the main title for the set of notes at the top.

2. Below the main title, describe what the set of notes is about in one or two sentences.

3. In the right-hand column, write sub-titles for the main points. Then write point-form notes below each sub-title.

4. Make small diagrams or sketches in the left column for each sub-title to help you remember the main ideas.

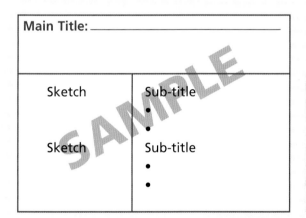

Main Title:	
Sketch	**Sub-title** • •
Sketch	**Sub-title** • •

Do ◆ Discuss ◆ Discover

1. In your notebook, write T-Notes about town streets and homes using the information on pages 64–66. Share your notes with a classmate and make any changes needed.

The Cathedral

Each Church region that was managed by a bishop had a huge church called a cathedral. Cathedrals were usually built in cities or towns.

Cathedrals took vast amounts of effort, time, and money to build. However, they were built to last forever. The builders wished to praise God by creating a perfect place for God on Earth. That is why cathedrals were larger and more beautiful than any other building.

Cathedrals took so long to build that the architect might not live to see it finished. The people who donated the money also often died before it was done.

Styles of Cathedrals

Between 900 and 1150, many stone cathedrals of Europe were built in the **Romanesque** style of architecture. Doors and windows with rounded arches at the top were set in thick stone walls.

Durham Cathedral in the north of England is a Romanesque-style building.

Inside, thick columns supported the heavy roofs. Round arches held up curved ceilings, called vaults. The amount of light that could enter the building was limited. Carved decoration and coloured stone made them beautiful.

Many medieval churches built in England after the mid-1100s were in the **Gothic** style.

The cathedral in Salisbury, England, is a beautiful Gothic-style building.

The walls and pillars of Gothic churches were narrower and taller than the Romanesque style. Tall stained-glass windows let in beams of light. New types of roof support rose from the tops of the pillars. The vaulted ceiling was high above the floor.

Buttresses

Extra support was needed to help balance the weight of the heavy roof on the thinner, taller walls and columns of Gothic churches. **Buttresses** were supports built against outside walls to strengthen them.

Buttresses that arch upward from a support are called flying buttresses.

Decorative Arts

Carvers and glass-workers used simple tools and great skill to create the beautiful decoration on cathedrals.

Carvers

Stone carvers decorated certain pieces of stone before the masons put them in place. They also created larger pieces of sculpture, such as

images of saints or pictures from Bible stories. Some cathedrals were covered with fine carving and statues.

There is detailed carving around the arch of this Romanesque door frame.

Medieval artists carved scenes and figures to decorate wooden furniture and wooden panelling in cathedrals.

Do ◆ Discuss ◆ Discover

1. As a class, discuss reasons why cathedrals were so large and everything so beautifully carved. Record the discussion points in your notebook.

Medieval Stained Glass

Stained-glass windows allowed light into churches and cathedrals. Windows usually showed scenes from Bible stories. This helped educate people, since few could read.

Pieces of coloured and clear glass were shaped to fit together inside a frame using glass-cutting tools. The images and beautiful colours were painted onto the cut pieces of glass with enamel paint. Then the pieces were baked at a high heat to make the colour permanent. The same process is used today.

The pieces of glass were fitted together between strips of lead and wedged into the frame. Hot lead was used to fix the strips together.

Making a Stained-Glass Window

You will need
- pencil and paper
- sheet of acetate
- set of permanent markers
- construction paper

1. Draw a design on paper for a stained-glass window. Use heavy lines to show where pieces of glass are joined by pieces of lead. Use light lines to show details in the picture. Make notes about the colours you will use.

2. Place the sheet of acetate over your design and trace the heavy lines in black permanent marker. Trace the details within the "pieces" of glass with finer lines. Colour your design with permanent markers.

3. Cut a frame for your stained-glass window from construction paper. Fasten the acetate to the back of the frame, and display it so the light shines through it.

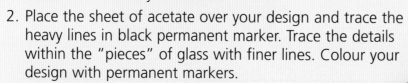

A Chance for a New Life

Margaret stood behind her father's shoulder and listened as the family talked with Roland. Her father had worked for Roland last summer when they rebuilt the castle walls after the siege. Roland had said then that he hoped Father would work with him again. Today he had arrived from York. It sounded as if he wanted them all to move there.

"I'm not sure, Roland," said her mother. "It's a long way. I've always lived in this village. We have this house, and a garden, and hens and geese. We keep our animals on the common land, and we know all the people here."

"But, Mother," interrupted Dan, "you know that Father says I am good at working stone. There is little to learn around here except making repairs and building walls. I'd like a chance to work on an important new building. A cathedral in York would be a wonderful chance for me."

"What do you think, Father?" asked Margaret's second brother, Arthur. Arthur was a quiet boy who was clever with his hands. He was carving a family of wooden dolls for Margaret.

Father was quiet for a moment. "There are many things to think about. It would be steady work with good pay. If the three of us all worked on the project, the family would prosper. The stone masons' guild has a hall there. Roland says he will recommend the boys as apprentices. That could not happen here in the village."

Dan and Arthur looked eager, but Margaret's mother bent her head to hide her disappointment.

"Hilda," Father said softly. "There will be others who have left their villages and are looking for new friends. You could take the hens and the red calf. We will be able to afford to buy some of our food, and you will have more time for weaving. It will be all right. You will see."

Mother smiled reluctantly. Margaret knew then that they would be going to York, a busy town with streets, shops, and many more people. She would learn to weave, too, and they would make the most beautiful cloth in York.

The Town of Ludlow

A castle was built at Ludlow, England, and the town was planned at the same time.

King William I of England gave manor land to one of his knights, Walter de Lacy. Between 1086 and 1094, Walter's son Roger de Lacy built Ludlow Castle.

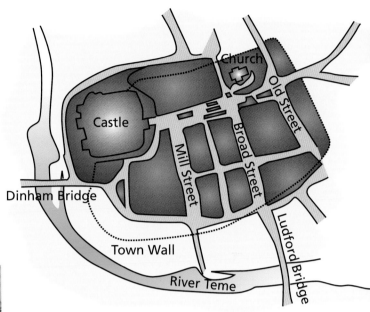

The town of Ludlow was built in several stages within the castle wall.

The ruins of Ludlow Castle look over Ludlow today.

It was a good site, with high cliffs on three sides. It controlled the crossing of the River Teme. There was a good view of the surrounding countryside. These were important when defending the castle and town in a war.

Ludlow was a planned town, rather than a village that became a town. Markets and fairs helped it grow. Many merchants and craftspeople came to visit and decided to live there. The town grew in wealth, and larger buildings were constructed. A church built in 1199 still stands today.

Ludlow

- All streets were originally inside the castle walls.

- The streets were laid out to be straight and were named.

- The house plots were narrow and long (10 metres wide) because land inside the castle walls was limited.

- houses were built mainly of wood, and fire was a constant threat.

- Pasture, farm fields, and woodland were outside the castle walls.

- Ludlow became a major trading centre where goods were collected and distributed.

- The cloth trade, based on English wool, was Ludlow's most important industry. Water mills on the River Teme provided power.

- The Ludlow townspeople applied to the king for a town charter. It was granted by the king in 1459.

Using Your Learning

Understanding Concepts

1. Choose a form of note-making and make notes on cathedrals from pages 68–70. Share with another student and make any changes necessary.

2. Identify vocabulary from Chapter 5 to add to the Vocabulary section of your notebook. Add diagrams or sketches to help you remember the words and their meanings.

Developing Inquiry/Research and Communication Skills

3. Imagine you are moving from a medieval village to a town or city. Write a letter describing how you feel about moving. What are you looking forward to and what are you concerned about?

Applying Skills and Concepts in Various Contexts

4. Choose one of the following topics:
   - a modern church
   - houses today
   - businesses today

   a) Fold a blank paper in half. On the front, use pictures and words to describe your topic.

   b) On the inside, use pictures and words to describe your topic in medieval times.

Medieval Times Project

1. Review the game board sketch and notes for instructions and make changes to the sketch if needed. You will be testing your game as a rough design before starting the final artwork.

2. Discuss and collect materials needed to construct the final game board and the other materials such as game pieces.

3. Discuss and decide on the best way to use the information being collected from each chapter. If you will use the information as questions and answers, continue to collect it this way. If it will be in a different form, begin to revise the information you have already collected.

4. Identify key information about medieval towns and cities from Chapter 5. Include it in your game.

Chapter 6
Town and City Life

People often moved to towns and cities to find a different kind of life than the one to which they were born. Some became successful and wealthy. Others remained poor. People formed groups called **guilds** to support and control their occupations.

Focus on Learning

In this chapter you will learn about
- cloth and clothing styles worn by townspeople
- sanitation and health in towns
- occupations of townspeople
- cost of living in towns
- guilds
- town markets, fairs, and entertainment
- descriptive writing
- books and education
- town law and justice

Vocabulary

guild	apprentice
sanitation	journeyman
contagious	parchment
proclamation	illuminations

Cloth and Clothing

The most important cloth in medieval England was wool. Some linen was also produced. The wealth of many English towns was based on sales of fleece from sheep and wool cloth.

Wool

1 shear sheep

2 card wool

3 spin thread

4 weave cloth

5 dye cloth

Linen

Linen was produced from fibres in the stems of the flax plant. The plants were soaked in water and left to rot to soften them. Then, they were beaten with paddles. This separated the stems into long fibres. These fibres were spun into thread, which was woven into cloth.

The finest linen fibres made thin, soft cloth. The cloth was bleached in the sun to make it white. Coarser fibres were made into rougher, less expensive linen.

Elsewhere...

Silk had been made in China for almost 3000 years before Europe's medieval times. For centuries, the method of making it was kept a secret. A silk industry began in the Middle East around 550 because of trade with China. Most silk sold in Europe was imported from traders in Constantinople (now Istanbul, Turkey). Silkworms could not be raised in Europe because of the climate.

Clothing Styles

The clothing of townspeople reflected their social group and wealth. Former serfs, poor people, and labourers wore clothing similar to villagers' clothing. The families of successful merchants and craftspeople wore more elaborate clothing.

Travellers and traders came to towns. They wore new styles from southern Europe and sold fabrics from Asia. Some wealthy townspeople began to wear velvet and silk, fur, tightly fitted clothes, hanging sleeves, trailing hems on dresses, and elaborate hats and headdresses, like those shown in Chapter 4.

Sometimes, nobles passed laws forbidding ordinary people from wearing the same styles as the nobility. These laws were usually ignored.

Do ◊ Discuss ◊ Discover

1. Make a three-column organizer. Label the columns: Villagers, Townspeople, Nobles. Compare the clothing of each using pages 22, 48, 49, and 76. Record your findings in the organizer.

Sanitation and Health

Medieval towns and cities were crowded and dirty. Clean water was almost impossible to get. Disease spread quickly. Elderly people, young children, and women giving birth often died.

Sanitation

Medieval people did not understand the importance of good **sanitation** for preventing diseases. Disposing of human and animal wastes and garbage was a constant problem for towns. Streams and wells became polluted. Towns made laws about where certain types of businesses could be located. Some sources of smell, pollution, and disease were leather tanners, dyers, and slaughter-houses. Water pollution is a problem that towns continue to face today.

Leprosy

Leprosy was one of the most feared diseases in medieval times. People who had leprosy had to live outside the city walls in leper houses. They could not go barefoot, wash in a stream or spring, or enter a mill, church, bakehouse, or inn. Because they could not work, they had to beg for alms. They carried a begging bowl and made a sound with a clapper. That told everyone a leper was near.

Hospitals

The word hospital came from the word hospice. Hospices were first started by convents and monasteries as places for pilgrims to stay. They were also used by elderly, needy, and sick people.

All of the sick people in the hospice rested, ate, lived, and prayed in the same large room.

Doctors

Wealthy people paid doctors to look after them, usually in their homes. Medieval doctors had less medical technology than doctors do today. Some were able to learn knowledge from medical writings in ancient Greek and Arabic.

Doctors examined patients and took samples of urine and blood. They asked questions about how patients felt. Some doctors could do operations on the body or the skull. However, patients often died from infection.

Doctors used alcohol or strong drugs to dull their patients' pain. They knew how to set broken bones and stitch up wounds. However, they did not understand how **contagious** diseases spread from one person to another.

Doctors used bloodletting, or bleeding, to cure certain types of illness. It was believed that too much blood caused a person to be sick. Leeches might be put onto a person's skin to remove some blood. Otherwise, the doctor might bleed the sick person by cutting open a vein.

Dentists

Dentistry was practised in medieval times. Dentists did fillings for those who could pay for them. A dentist could make a false tooth from bone and place it in a patient's mouth if he or she could afford it. Poor people went to a tooth puller at the fair or the blacksmith to have bad teeth pulled.

Do ◊ Discuss ◊ Discover

1. Find the list in your notebook you made for question 1 on page 65. Add more causes of pollution to these notes from information on pages 77 and 78.

Townspeople

In early medieval times, most people were involved in farming and producing food. Families were often self-sufficient for their basic needs. Later, most townspeople earned their livings doing other kinds of work.

People's houses, clothing, and possessions all had to be made, cleaned, and repaired. Most people did some of these things for themselves. Some paid other townspeople or traders for products and services.

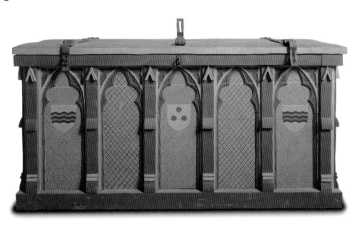

Occupations				
ale-mistress	candlemaker	furrier	lawyer	stone carver
apothecary	carpenter	glazier	locksmith	tanner
architect	carter	*(glass-maker)*	magistrate	teacher
artist	doctor	goldsmith	merchant	thatcher
baker	draper	grocer	miller	tooth puller
banker	*(cloth-seller)*	inn-keeper	musician	town crier
barber	dressmaker	jeweller	priest	watch captain
blacksmith	dyer	joiner	scribe	weaver
brewer	entertainer	labourer	servant	
butcher	fuller	laundress	shoemaker	

Do ◊ Discuss ◊ Discover

1. Make an organizer titled Occupations with the following categories: Food, Clothing, Homes, Services.

   a) List examples of each from the chart on this page.

   b) Circle the occupations that still exist today.

Cost of Living

The following prices and earnings are based on records kept in the 1200s. They were found in bailiffs' records and farm and manor accounts. One shilling was worth 12 pence.

Building a house

2 masons for 6 days' work
. . . . 2 1/2 pence a day each

2 carpenters for 4 days' work
. . . . 3 pence a day each

thatcher for 4 days' work. . . . 3 pence a day

Running a home

1 pound (454 g) of soap . . . . 1 penny

1 pound candles . . . . 1 1/2 pence

12 silver spoons. . . . . . . 2 shillings, 4 pence

1 yard (9/10 m) of linen. . . . . . . 3 1/4 pence

carpet with coat of arms of England
. . . . 20 shillings

A miller received 5 shillings a year in income. The candles were worth over a week's income for a miller. The silver spoons were worth almost half a year's income.

The carpet was bought for 20 shillings by a nobleman, the Earl of Clare. That was nearly half of a castle priest's annual income of 40 shillings and 2 pence a year.

Food

1 pound cloves. . . . . 10 shillings

1 pound pepper . . . . 9 pence

120 eggs. . . . . 2 1/2 pence

1 gallon (4 1/2 L) butter . . . . . 4 1/2 pence

A carpenter earned 3 pence a day for 4 days' work. He could afford eggs and butter. The Earl of Clare could easily afford luxuries such as cloves and pepper (spices).

Coins like these silver pennies (pence) could be clipped in halves or quarters to give them lower values.

The Town Crier

"Hear ye, hear ye!" This was the town crier's signal that he had some news to communicate. Town criers called out the news of the day. People gathered around to listen. This took the place of modern newspapers, radio, and television.

Proclamations were public messages that affected everybody, such as a change to a law or a tax. They might be read by a town official or someone who represented the king.

Guilds

Medieval guilds were trade organizations. Many guilds were made up of people who had the same occupation. There were also guilds of merchants who bought and sold a certain kind of product. Guilds controlled prices and set up trading rules. They set the standard for the quality of work expected in a product.

A dyer's apprentices are working in the business learning his skills.

Vintners' Guild

Guilds controlled who could receive training in an occupation. A person had to be accepted by the guild as an **apprentice** in order to train as a skilled worker. An apprentice lived in the home of the master craftsperson who was his teacher. The average period of training was seven years. Some guilds accepted women as members, but most did not.

After training, the apprentice had to submit a large project called a masterpiece to the guild council. If it was approved, the apprentice received the rank of **Journeyman**. Journeymen moved around getting a variety of experience rather than working for the same master. Some skilled journeymen eventually gained the rank of Master. Then, they could teach apprentices themselves.

Salters' Guild

A huge number of guilds were organized. Just a few examples were weavers, candle makers, bell ringers, and road menders. Some guilds were very important to the business life of towns. These powerful guilds influenced the way towns and cities were run.

Cloth Dyers' Guild

Apprenticeship is still common in trades like carpentry, plumbing, and welding. It combines on-the-job training with periods of schoolwork. Apprentices have exams at different stages of training. They no longer live with the family of their employer.

Markets and Fairs

Towns and cities had to get a licence from the king to hold markets and fairs.

Markets were held once or twice a week in the town square. People got up very early in the morning to set up their portable stalls and display their products. Others arrived from the country with produce to sell.

Candles, knives, needles, eggs, vegetables, honey, bread, freshly brewed ale, and shoes were just some of the things for sale at the market.

Medieval people advertized their goods and services with their voices. Their calls and chants added to the noise of the market.

The Fair

Fairs were special markets held once or twice a year. They attracted merchants and traders from great distances. Fairs were usually held for trading in a particular product. For example, farmers bought special animals at livestock fairs to improve their herds.

There were other attractions at the fair besides buying and selling. There were food stalls for people to get things like hot pies, sweet tarts, and ale. Certain services could also be found at a fair, such as tooth pullers and scribes.

People also went to be entertained. There might be stilt walkers, singers, jugglers, tumblers, performing animals, and puppets.

Some people also liked to gamble or place bets as they watched more violent activities like wrestling or bear-baiting. The Church disapproved of gambling.

Do ◊ Discuss ◊ Discover

1. With a partner, write and practise two chants advertizing different products or services at a fair.

Entertainment

Plays were a popular part of the celebrations of religious holy days. They were usually put on by the guilds. Local people acted in them every year.

Some towns put on a set of plays telling a long series of Bible stories. The whole set could take many days. Sometimes scenes took place on the wide cathedral steps. Other groups acted the scenes on flat wagons that were pulled through the town. The plays often used special effects. For example, pails of water might be dumped over the stage during the telling of the great flood in the story of Noah's Ark.

Mummers provided another type of entertainment. Local serfs and freemen wore masks representing animals and imaginary beings. They put on skits and mimes based on stories from ancient times. There was usually a dramatic sword fight, dancing, and chanting. Mummers entertained at special occasions for gifts of food and pennies.

Travelling minstrels and troubadours also entertained in towns. They sang about brave knights, beautiful ladies, and events happening in kingdoms far away.

Puppeteers travelled around, entertaining at fairs and in castles and manor houses. Puppet characters often included clowns, kings, animals, and a doctor to bring everybody back to life at the end.

Puppets have been a popular type of entertainment since long before medieval times.

Do ◆ Discuss ◆ Discover

1. Draw a graphic organizer in the shape of a theatre stage or puppet theatre. Title it Medieval Entertainment. Make notes on pages 82 and 83 under the headings: Travelling Performers, Local Performers. Add sketches of medieval performers to help you remember them.

Descriptive Writing

1. Descriptive writing uses words to create an experience that looks, smells, sounds, tastes, and feels real to the reader.

Sense	Example
Taste	the ocean wave's salty spray
Touch	the cold slap of the waves
Smell	the smell of wet wool from her scarf
Sight	The iron grey of the sea reflected the dark sky.
Hearing	The dog at her feet panted as the wind howled.

2. Good descriptive writing appeals to the reader's emotions. Words can be used to create a mood.

Mood	Example
lonely	A single seagull cried above the empty sea.
excited	Her heart thumped wildly when she saw the boat.

3. Descriptive writing portrays action in a way that the reader can imagine exactly what is happening. The reader can follow the sequence of action as events occur.

Example

The boat lurched sideways and rocked wildly up and down when she fell into the water. The dog threw himself out of the boat after her.

4. Descriptive writing adds details to give a clearer picture of a setting, a person, an action, or the way people act towards each other.

Example

She knew her boat was a little leaky. However, she hadn't noticed how much the boards had shrunk. Water started to show along the seams. A stream of water streaked across the bottom.

Do ◊ Discuss ◊ Discover

1. Read the story The Fall Fair on page 85. Discuss with a partner examples of descriptive writing in this story.

2. As an individual, choose a role or topic from pages 75–83. Imagine yourself in that time and place. Write a 2–3 paragraph description of what you are experiencing.

The Fall Fair

The sun was glancing across the tops of the town's slate and thatch roofs. However, the early morning air still felt cool. Jane and Harold were excited as they set out from their house. Hugo, the family's servant, was with them to carry packages and make sure they were safe. There were many strangers in town for the fall Cloth Fair. Father worried if they went out alone.

"Hurry up, Harold," said Jane. She was clutching a square of dress fabric in her hand. She wanted a piece of trim to match her new yellow silk dress and feared all the nice colours would be gone.

"I'm coming," complained Harold. His legs were shorter than hers and he couldn't keep up. "I have important errands, too. I must find a scribe to write to James in Oxford. I asked Brother Alfred, but he did not have time. I shall find someone at the Fair to do it." Jane smiled. She also missed their older brother who was away at university.

They hurried down Candlestick Lane. The smell of smoke from morning fires mixed with the smell of hot wax and tallow. Smells of fish from the next street and slops in the open gutter nearly overpowered them. As Jane and Harold turned a corner, they saw a shop selling meat pies and cheeses piled high. The smell of bread came from the bakery, along with the sweet smell of currant buns.

As they got closer to the fair, there were more townspeople and country people in the streets. The children also saw many strangers. Some were wearing elegant fashions and fabrics, flowing robes, and strange hats. Father had said that traders from Bruges and Venice were to be there, and Moors from southern Spain.

The glowing colours of the cloth on the stall of a cloth trader made Jane blink. The merchant ran a piece of trim through his fingers and held it up for the breeze to catch it. Peacock and scarlet silk and threads of gold glittered in the sun. She looked down when Harold pulled at her hand. He wanted to find a scribe first, before the fair was too crowded.

Books and Education

Machines for making copies of books were not used in Europe until after 1455. Books were written and copied by hand. They were written on **parchment** using quill pens made from goose feathers. Parchment was animal skin carefully scraped until it was thin, smooth, and dry. It was very expensive.

Very special books had full-page images and many tiny illustrations in the spaces where there was no writing. The first letter of each new piece of writing was large, elaborate, and decorated with tiny pictures. These were called **illuminations**. Bright colours and a thin layer of gold called gold leaf were often used.

Most book copying was done by monks. Monasteries often had libraries of books. If a wealthy noble wanted a book, he or she would pay the monastery to make a copy. Some books took many years to finish. Most books were about religious subjects. Others were about medicine, astronomy (the stars), and law. These were rarely illuminated.

Universities

During medieval times, universities were established in centres such as Oxford and Paris. Young men who already had their basic education went there to study. Medicine, religion, the arts, philosophy, and law were the usual subjects. Students entered university at 14 and received their first degree at 22.

Legacy

Students at modern universities usually begin their studies at about 18 years of age.

Making an Illuminated Nameplate

You will need

- pencil, eraser, ruler
- white paper
- felts/paints
- gold acrylic paint

1. Plan your nameplate by doing several sketches. Use about one-third of the space for the illuminated capital letter. Choose a style of lettering from reference books or the Internet, or make up your own. Sketch in the remaining letters so they fit the space.

2. Research examples of illuminated letters and medieval book decoration. Choose a theme for your nameplate. Some examples are village life, knights and ladies, animals of the woodland, jesters and dancers, and imaginary creatures.

3. Carefully draw the illuminated letter. Outline the other letters of your name and fill them in with a colour.

4. Sketch and colour all of the decoration and picture parts of the nameplate.

5. When the nameplate is completely dry, carefully add gold paint to form rich accents.

6. You can put your nameplate in a frame or glue it onto a cardboard backing for display.

Town Law and Justice

Towns had few prisons for law-breakers. Trials for wrong-doing happened quickly. Townspeople were usually tried by a town official or they were brought before the town council. Fines were paid for many crimes. Towns and cities used this money to pay for services like the watch.

People could be expelled from town or hanged for serious offences. A thief might lose a hand or be hanged. Shopkeepers who cheated the public by not measuring correctly or over-charging were punished in public. The stocks were commonly used.

Nobles or members of a noble household were not usually tried by the town officials. The town council could take a complaint to the lord. In very serious cases, they could appeal to the king or queen.

Churchmen, monks, and nuns were never judged by town officials either. The Church had a separate system of laws and courts for its own people.

Medieval Lawyers

After 1300, the first English law schools were started in the city of London. Good students were chosen to train as lawyers. Lawyers argued for people's rights in the king's court.

Do ◊ Discuss ◊ Discover

1. Review pages 33, 51, and 88.
   List 2 similarities in law and justice in the village, castle, and town in your notebook. Share your list with a classmate.

Using Your Learning

Understanding Concepts

1. Make a web in your notes like the one shown below. Complete the web to show how religion was an important part of town and city life.

2. Identify vocabulary from Chapter 6 to add to the Vocabulary section of your notebook. Add diagrams or sketches to help you remember the words and their meanings. Add more parts to the web as needed.

Developing Inquiry/Research and Communication Skills

3. Research one of the occupations listed on page 79. In your notebook, write four or five interesting things you discover about this occupation.

Applying Skills and Concepts in Various Contexts

4. Imagine that you could only buy fresh food once or twice a week. You don't have a refrigerator to keep things fresh. Ask the food shopper(s) in your house to tell you about the ways he or she buys food. Compare it with the way people shopped in medieval times. Use the information on page 50 to help you.

5. Choose a topic from this chapter. Work in pairs to create a short, descriptive story to read aloud *or* create finger or stick puppets and write a one-minute play to present to your class.

6. Locate the work you did for question 1 on pages 65 and 78. Then, draw a comparison organizer in your notes to compare pollution in medieval times with Canada today.

Medieval Times Project

1. Review the game board design and the game instructions. Ask someone outside your group to read the instructions and then give feedback on how they think the game is played. Did they understand the way the game is played? Revise the instructions until they are clear.

2. Identify key information about town and city life from Chapter 6. Use the form you have chosen to include it in the game.

Chapter 7
A Medieval Kingdom

In a medieval kingdom, the king was the ruler. The nobles in the kingdom were vassals of the king. They owed loyalty and service to him. Nobles, kings, and Church leaders sometimes disagreed about rights and taxes. Some disagreements led to conflict, and some led to change.

Focus on Learning

In this chapter you will learn about
• the political structure in medieval times
• the roles of a king
• the roles of a queen
• methods of warfare
• the Magna Carta
• cause and effect

Vocabulary

allegiance	coronation
alliance	heir
consensus	regent
inherit	Magna Carta

The Kingdom

A medieval kingdom included all the land governed by a king and the king's vassals. Most medieval kingdoms were smaller than modern countries.

> A country is an area with an agreed-upon boundary and its own central government.

In medieval times, wars among kings and powerful nobles were common. Wars changed the boundaries of kingdoms. The winner of a war often took over the loser's land.

For example, William, Duke of Normandy, landed in England with an army in 1066. He defeated Harold, the English king, and became king of England. King William I of England is often referred to as William the Conquerer. He divided England among the noble knights who were his vassals.

Vassals swore **allegiance** to the king. They promised loyalty and support. The king often needed the armies of his vassals to fight with his army in wars. They helped him defend the kingdom or take over additional land.

Vassals often provided their own horses and armour when they fought as knights in the king's army. They brought foot-soldiers and archers with them. They also paid taxes from the income of their manors to support the king's army.

Some of a king's vassals were wealthy, powerful nobles who were strong enough to challenge his right to govern. Kings had to carefully balance different forces in the kingdom so they continued to hold power.

Alan of Brittany swears loyalty to William I, as one of his vassals.

Elsewhere...

In the north-eastern United States in the 1400s, a group of Iroquoian First Nations formed an **alliance**. An alliance is an agreement that benefits all sides. The nations agreed not to make war on each other. They agreed to meet and discuss issues that affected them all. There was no single leader of the alliance. The group of leaders made decisions by **consensus**. That meant they all had to agree on a solution before it was accepted.

The King

In medieval England, the king was the ruler of a kingdom.

Kings usually chose advisors to assist them. However, a king did not have to take their advice. If royal advisors disagreed with the king, they might be ignored, sent away, or even punished.

Most kings **inherited** their lands and title from a dying king. If a king had no son, a daughter could be named queen. However, this did not happen during the medieval period.

During the **coronation** ceremony, the new king received the crown from the most important Church leader in the kingdom. Holy oil was put on the king's head to show God's approval.

Royal Allies

Kings formed friendships if they thought it would benefit them. These alliances meant they could count on each other in times of war. They agreed to allow trade goods and traders to pass through their lands, for a price. They visited each other and sent each other elaborate gifts. Sometimes these friendships broke down and kings declared war on each other.

King David II of Scotland and King Edward III of England are shaking hands as equals.

A medieval king is being crowned and given the symbols of authority.

A King's Ransom

If a king was captured in battle, a huge ransom could be demanded for his return. In 1193, King Richard I of England, known as Richard *Coeur de Lion* (Lionheart), was captured. A ransom of 150 000 marks (about $23 million today) was demanded for his safe return. His vassals had to raise the money by selling land, jewels, and other possessions.

Roles of a Queen

A queen might be the wife of a king or the ruler of a kingdom that had no ruling king.

Wife of the King

As wife of the king, the queen had many duties:

- having children so there would be an **heir** to the throne when the king died

- keeping the accounts and planning with the steward what food, medicines, and other supplies were needed

- arranging the education of the noble children who lived at court, teaching manners and the skills of running a noble household

- ensuring the castle servants could be trusted to keep order

- planning banquets, clothing, and entertainment

A queen also spent time doing needlework, listening to music, and reading. She learned arithmetic so she could check accounts. A queen might be more literate than the king, who had scribes to read and write for him.

A Ruling Queen

In medieval times in England, a queen might rule as **regent**

- if the king died, until the king's eldest son was old enough to rule

- if the king was absent, such as away at war

Most people in medieval times believed the ruler needed to be a man. They felt that powerful nobles would fight among themselves and try to take over unless there was a male ruler.

Queen Elizabeth II became a ruling queen in 1952. Her coronation was in 1953.

Do ◊ Discuss ◊ Discover

1. Create a web in your notebook of the roles of kings and queens. You may add colour or small images to your web to help you remember points.

Eleanor of Aquitaine

Eleanor of Aquitaine's father, the Duke of Aquitaine, died in 1137. She inherited a large, valuable piece of land, shown on the map on the right, when she was 15 years old.

King Louis VII of France married Eleanor. He knew that he would then control her lands. The income from them and the busy seaport of Bordeaux added to his power. Eleanor was queen of France for 15 years, but the marriage was unhappy. In 1152, the Church permitted their divorce.

Many noblemen wished to marry Eleanor. She chose Henry, Duke of Anjou. He became King Henry II of England two years later.

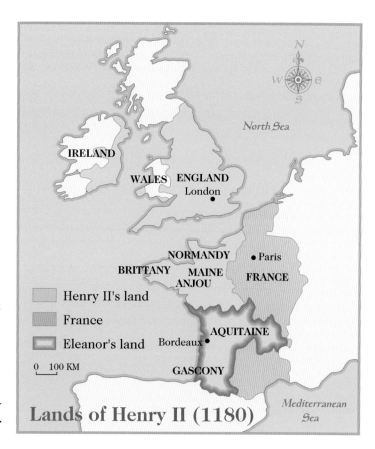

Lands of Henry II (1180)

Eleanor of Aquitaine and Henry II are buried in Fontevrault Abbey in Anjou.

Both the king and queen were used to having power, and they did not always agree. Eventually she returned to France. He imprisoned her in a castle to keep her away from his court. She encouraged their sons to rebel against her husband.

Eleanor remained in France for 16 years. When her son Richard became king, he made her regent in England. She ruled on his behalf while he took part in wars elsewhere. After he died, Eleanor's youngest son, John, became the king of England. Eleanor retired to a convent in France, where she remained until her death.

Robin hood

On a cool, sunny day in autumn, Robin hood and Will Scarlet stood under the great oak trees of Sherwood Forest.

"I'm pleased to see we are well-provided for the winter, Will," said Robin, smiling. "I am content that we shall not starve. We are surrounded by the king's deer." This was one of the reasons Robin and his companions were hunted by the sheriff as outlaws. They did not respect the king's right to all of the forests in England.

King John was disliked by many of his subjects. he made huge demands for taxes to pay for wars that he could not win. Men were forced off their land for not being able to pay the king's taxes. Robin's band of outlaws grew even larger.

Suddenly, Robin and Will heard shouts and cries of pain. They slipped through the forest to a clearing. There, they saw the sheriff's men scuffling with young Alan Ford, a serf from the nearby village. Two dead hares lay on the ground beside a sack. Alan had been lucky with his snares that morning, but not lucky enough to escape unnoticed. "Call the men," said Robin.

Will blew a long note on his horn. The sheriff's men in the clearing tensed and looked around nervously. half a dozen green-clad men appeared like shadows. Robin drew a circle in the air. The men fitted arrows to their bows, circled the clearing, and surrounded the serf and his captors. As Robin stepped forward, his men drew back their bowstrings.

"Come," said Robin. "Is it fair for four of you to take one poor serf?"

"You know the law," snarled the leader. "There lies the evidence. Poaching is a hanging offence these days."

"Nay," said Robin, "there will be no hanging today. My men and I say the rabbits are ours. We gave him the right of them. Unhand him, or face the effect of your bad judgement."

The sheriff's men were outnumbered. They were not foolish, so they freed Alan. The shocked youth stumbled towards Robin. he was grateful to be alive, but he knew that he would not be able to return to his farm.

"Don't forget to bring our supper, lad," said Robin, pointing to the hares. "I think it's your turn to cook tonight."

Warfare

Conflict among kings and nobles often led to war. Battles were very expensive. A king or noble had to raise huge amounts of money to fight a war. Battles were avoided if possible.

The technology of warfare changed as new methods were developed.

Siege

A castle was under siege when an army surrounded the walls and prevented supplies from reaching it. Attackers often burned homes and fields around the castle. They took over the local food supply and sometimes poisoned the castle's water source. They expected the defenders to surrender or starve. Sometimes attackers had to stop the siege without taking the castle.

Attacking a Castle

There were different ways of attacking a castle that did not surrender:

1. draining the moat and filling it with earth to reach the walls, to undermine them so they collapsed

2. shooting from behind huge wooden shields called pavises

3. using an attack tower to reach over the castle walls

4. battering the wall with stones using catapults

5. using a huge catapult called a trebuchet (treh byou shet). The heavy weight on one end was lowered and the catapult loaded with stones, a dead animal, or fire. When the trebuchet was released, the load was flung over the wall.

By 1400, cannons were being used against castles. By 1450, they were large enough to knock holes in castle walls.

Battering rams were used to knock down the gate. A shelter of wet hides on a wooden frame protected fighters from boiling oil or water thrown from above.

Open Battle

Battles were fought between armies on open ground in summer. Knights fought on horseback. They rode into the ranks of the opposing army. Armour gave them some protection. They fought with swords, lances, and maces (clubs).

Foot soldiers wore less armour than mounted knights. They fought hand-to-hand with swords, battle axes, and maces. Archers stood behind the front line and shot arrows towards the ranks of the other side.

Battles could last for several hours. Many thousands died. At the end of the battle, badly injured soldiers were killed instead of being left to suffer.

After a castle or a town was captured, or a battle lost, many of the defeated people might be killed by the winners. Knights and nobles were usually held for ransom.

> An expert longbowman could shoot six times in one minute. Crossbows could shoot only once a minute but were strong enough to pierce armour.

Do ♦ Discuss ♦ Discover

1. In your notebook, write T-notes about warfare. Look back to page 67 for information on T-notes.

The Magna Carta

England was in trouble in the time of King John. The country had been involved in costly wars. Rather than gaining more land and wealth, they had lost some valuable lands. King John set extra taxes on both manors and towns. He allowed towns to purchase charters so he could collect taxes from them. This income had once been paid to the lords. He also angered the Church.

A Bishop

"The king has no right to interfere with the Church. He tried to tell us who should be named the head of the Church in England. That is a Church matter, not his to rule.

"He quarreled with the pope. The pope closed all English churches for a year to punish John. The king has made everyone suffer for his stubbornness."

King John

"It is my right as king to make decisions. I will not have my vassals tell me how I should reign as king.

"I have to think of the good of the whole kingdom, not just the desires of this or that person. I need more men to protect this country's lands. It costs a lot to feed an army. I shall raise the taxes when I need to."

A Noble

"King John does not consult with us or listen to his noble advisors. He wants all the money from our high courts. Fines paid for wrongdoings are part of our right, yet he demands them. He expects us to accept his decisions without complaining!

"The king should have to call an assembly of nobles when he wants to raise money. The assembly needs to agree to his plans. The nobles will make sure he keeps his promises."

A Merchant

"King John puts men in prison without a trial by their peers. We have had the right of trial for one hundred years.

"He also takes away some of our city charter rights. We are supposed to decide how much money to pay in taxes, but he interferes in trade by wanting more."

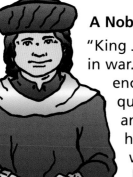

A Noble

"King John is not a good leader in war. He does not fight hard enough. He wastes his time quarrelling with his nobles and other rulers. His quarrels have lost us much land and wealth in France that belonged to England."

A Merchant

"My husband worked hard to establish a trade in silk when he was alive. After he died, I kept the business going. However, traders from the east do not wish to come here because they have to pay all those extra import taxes."

After many attempts to pursuade King John to change his ways, in 1215 the English nobles forced him to sign the **Magna Carta** in a field called Runnymede, west of London. *Magna Carta* is Latin for "Great Charter."

The legal right not to be put in prison without a trial is a result of the conditions in the Magna Carta.

Some Conditions in the Magna Carta

1. The rights of the nobles shall be respected.

2. No tax shall be owing except those agreed to by the council of the assembly.

3. No free person shall be taken or imprisoned except by legal judgement based on the law of the land.

4. A trial shall be held within a reasonable time after imprisonment.

5. All fines set in a manorial court shall belong to the lord of the manor.

6. The Church shall keep its rights and be free to appoint people to Church positions.

7. Merchants can trade without paying extra taxes.

8. Weights and measures shall be agreed upon by all.

Do ◊ Discuss ◊ Discover

1. Review pages 98 and 99. Make an organizer and use it to match the speakers with the conditions listed on this page. Which conditions in the list have not been stated by any of the speakers?

2. Condition 8 of the Magna Carta states that there should be a common system of weights and measurements. What advantages would this have?

Cause and Effect

You often hear the question "Why did that happen?" when students study an event of history or when people watch the news. To help answer the question, you need to understand what caused the event. There is usually more than one part to a situation that brings about an event. Also, events often cause something to change. This is the effect.

One way of helping to understand the situation is to use a Cause and Effect organizer.

1. Identify the cause(s). A cause is a reason that an event happens. There may be more than one cause of an event.

2. Describe the event that occurred. This is the action that took place because of the cause(s).

3. Outline the effects or changes that came about as consequences of the event.

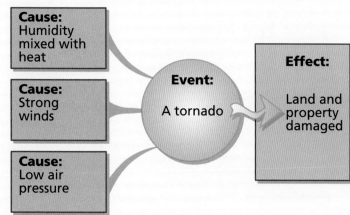

Cause: Humidity mixed with heat

Cause: Strong winds

Cause: Low air pressure

Event: A tornado

Effect: Land and property damaged

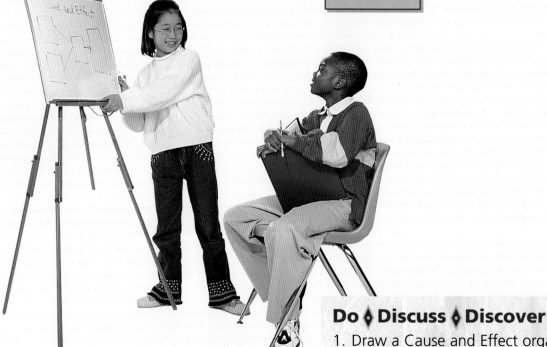

Do ◊ Discuss ◊ Discover

1. Draw a Cause and Effect organizer in your notebook. Use information from pages 98 and 99 to fill in the organizer. List the causes and the effects of the Magna Carta. Share and discuss your organizer with a classmate.

Using Your Learning

Understanding Concepts

1. Identify vocabulary from Chapter 7 to add to the Vocabulary section of your notebook. Add diagrams or sketches to help you remember the words and their meanings.

Developing Inquiry/Research and Communication Skills

2. In the library or on the Internet, find and read a legend or story related to the medieval period. Share it with a classmate.

3. Imagine you are the town crier who will be announcing the signing of the Magna Carta. Write the announcement in your own words. Remember to catch people's attention quickly and include important facts. Practise and present it to the class.

4. Design a poster advertising an archery competition for people interested in joining the King's Archers. Include what, when, where, why, and any other important information. Remember that most people could not read. Use visuals to get your message across.

Applying Skills and Concepts in Various Contexts

5. Discuss the following topic in groups of three.
   • How are government leaders chosen today?
   In your discussion, compare how governments are chosen today with the medieval kingdom.

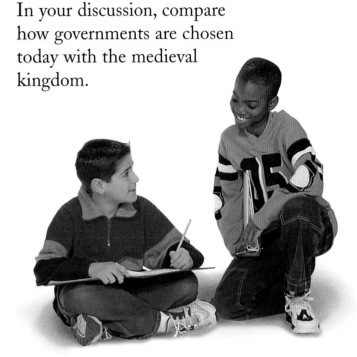

Medieval Times Project

1. Review the checklist of tasks that still need to be done.

2. Create a test copy of your game. Assign tasks; for example, writing out the instructions, making a clean rough copy of the game on newsprint, making or collecting a rough set of all of the other elements of the game. As a group, create the test version of your game.

3. When your group is ready, test the game by playing it. Make notes about changes you may need to make. Put them in your folder.

4. Identify key information about the medieval kingdom from Chapter 7. Use the form you have chosen to include it in the game.

Chapter 8
Life at Court

The king was surrounded by many people. Visitors brought requests and information. Guests and royal advisors attended banquets and entertainments dressed in fine clothing. Sometimes, the needs of the kingdom were more important than the king's personal wishes.

Focus on Learning

In this chapter you will learn about
- the royal court
- advisors and courtiers
- banquets
- clothing and goods
- entertainment
- Christmas at court
- the Church and the kingdom

Vocabulary

royal court   courtiers
petition   exchequer

The Royal Court

In medieval times, the **royal court** referred to two things:

- the king and his royal advisors and officials, who governed the kingdom
- the king's residence

Holding Court

The king had official working time, when court meetings were held. There was also much unofficial working time. People who attended banquets, hunting parties, and social events often wanted to talk about their concerns.

Life at court was very active. Nobles, Church leaders, and townspeople came to court to try to meet with the king. Many met first with a royal advisor or a family member whose opinion the king trusted.

People came with **petitions** (written requests) about town charters, taxes, armies, supplies, famine, the crops, and many other concerns. Sometimes they reported threats from enemies or unrest among the people.

It was important that the king knew what was happening in the kingdom. Advisors helped him to think about problems from different points of view.

On his royal seal, King William I holds symbols of his authority—a sword and an orb.

The Royal Residence

The main royal castle in England was usually in or near London. However, a king had other manors and castles around the country.

The king's court travelled around the kingdom. The king heard petitions in different places and tried to keep peace among the people. Family members, servants, dogs, clothing, horses, and supplies moved slowly from one place to another in a Royal Progress. Sometimes, they all stayed in the castle or manor house of a noble. This was an honour, but it was also expensive for the noble.

Royal Mail

Kings, nobles, and religious leaders wrote official letters to each other. These messages were sealed with the official seal and hand-delivered. Trusted servants travelled at top speed to deliver a royal letter.

Advisors and Courtiers

Many people lived at court. There were members of the royal family, royal advisors and officials, **courtiers**, and many servants. Courtiers included guests, ambassadors from other royal courts, ladies-in-waiting, and knights.

Trusted officials helped manage the kingdom. They were usually the king's most important noble vassals.

The justiciar kept order while the king passed judgement in his court. When the king was absent, the justiciar passed royal judgements. Stewards had this role on royal manors.

The chamberlain was the king's treasurer. He also looked after the royal bedchamber. Kings of earlier times had kept their valuables in the bedchamber. The chamberlain had to be trustworthy.

Servants looked after the needs of the family and guests, the castle, armoury, knights, and animals.

A medieval author is presenting a copy of his book to the king as other courtiers look on.

Royal Children

The eldest son of the king was his heir. He had to learn the skills of a ruler. Other sons would be expected to train as knights and learn to manage large land holdings.

The marriages of royal children were an essential way of creating or strengthening alliances with other kingdoms. These marriages were often arranged in childhood. A princess sometimes moved to the court of her royal husband as a child. She was educated and trained there in her role as a princess or queen. Princes usually went to other courts as pages.

The Exchequer

Twice a year, the king's sherrifs brought the taxes they had collected to the court treasury. Royal officials checked the tax money using a system called the **exchequer**. The tax coins were accounted for using the squares of a large checkered cloth. This system of taxation was started by King Henry I.

Do ◊ Discuss ◊ Discover

1. Describe in your notes the process by which a person might get a petition presented to the king.

Banquets

Banquets in the king's hall were elaborate, colourful, and noisy. Trumpets blew to announce the meal as the king and queen entered. Honoured guests sat with them at the high table.

Guests washed their hands with water poured from an ornamental pitcher by a servant.

A cupbearer served the king's wine. A royal taster tested his food for spoilage or poison.

The Food

There were several courses. Each had several dishes to choose from. Soups, cooked eels and fish, roasted goose, swans, and songbirds, and the meat of sheep and pig were common. Sauces and some vegetable dishes would be included.

Cooks tried to please the king and delight the guests. They made specially decorated dishes and surprises. For example, live birds might be covered with baked piecrust. When the crust was cut open, the birds flew out.

Fennel with Ginger

750 g trimmed, fresh fennel root, cleaned and cut in matchsticks

225 g onions, thickly sliced

7 mL of ground ginger

5 mL of powdered saffron

2 mL of salt

30 mL of olive oil

150 mL each of dry white wine and water

6 thick slices of coarse wholemeal bread (optional)

Stir first six ingredients together over medium heat. Then add liquids. Bring to a boil, and then simmer for 20–30 minutes until cooked but not mushy. Serve with roast meat or fried fish, or poured over a slice of bread on a plate.

– adapted from a recipe used by King Richard II's cooks

Do ◆ Discuss ◆ Discover

1. Re-read page 21 about medieval village food. In a Venn diagram in your notes, identify similarities and differences between food at court and in a medieval village.

Clothing and Goods

Royal families, courtiers, and officials wore expensive clothes and jewels. This showed their wealth and importance to visitors and ambassadors from other courts.

Trade with other kingdoms brought beautiful, expensive materials to people who could afford them. Furs, silk, velvet, fine weaving, jewels, decorated dishes and objects made of precious metal, art, and other goods were imported by wealthy rulers and nobles. As trade and travel increased, clothing and possessions became more elaborate.

Jewels and pearls were sewn onto both men's and women's clothing, headdresses, and hats. Rings and other jewellery were worn by both men and women.

Church leaders wore richly decorated robes with gold and silver embroidery.

Valuable personal items such as small boxes and hand-made books might be decorated with gold, jewels, carving, or painting. Royalty and wealthy nobles often owned religious items like crosses or paintings created by great artists.

Legacy

The Crown Jewels belong to the ruler sitting on the throne of the United Kingdom. They are official symbols of a ruling king or queen, not personal jewellery. The crown, sceptre, and orb are received at the coronation and used only at special events. They represent the ruler's authority. The Crown Jewels are kept in the Tower of London.

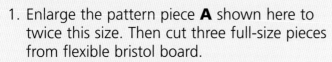

Making a Crown

You will need
- flexible bristol board
- scissors, tape, glue
- large paper clips
- gold or silver wrapping paper

You may want
- metallic paints
- coloured sparkles
- fake gems and pearls

1. Enlarge the pattern piece **A** shown here to twice this size. Then cut three full-size pieces from flexible bristol board.

2. Glue them together with 1 cm seams to form a single flat piece.

3. Wrap the crown around your head to check the length. You can adjust the size by overlapping the ends. Use the paper clips to hold it together.

4. Cut a piece of wrapping paper large enough to cover the flat crown, with overlaps. See diagram **B**.

5. Lay the flat crown on the back of the wrapping paper. Snip the paper every few centimetres around the base (as shown in **B**). Fold up the pieces and then tape them. Snip to the corners of the diamonds. Now fold and tape.

6. Use your imagination when decorating your crown. One method is to make three-dimensional "jewels" from cardboard. Paint the "setting" with metallic paint and glue on jewel-coloured sparkles. Glue the decorations to your crown.

A

(Cut 3)

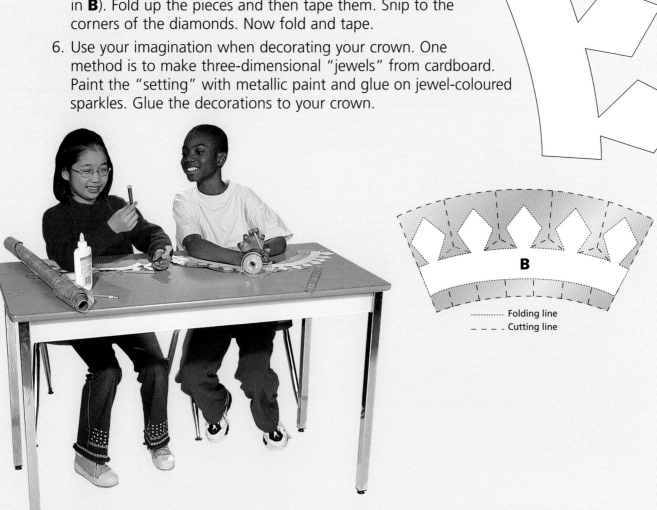

B

·········· Folding line
– – – – Cutting line

Entertainment

People at the royal court enjoyed watching and listening to entertainers, hunting, falconry, and playing games.

Music

Minstrels and troubadours were travelling musicians who entertained in royal courts, nobles' great halls, and at fairs. They sang ballads about kings, heroes, war, chivalry, and love. Medieval musical instruments included the lyre, gittern, harp, bagpipes, hurdy-gurdy organ, and drums.

Hunting

The royal forests of England belonged to the king. He and his guests hunted for sport as well as for food for the table. Horses and trained hunting dogs were valuable.

Falconry was popular in medieval times. The birds were valuable and took many hours to train. The noble hunter sent the falcon or hawk into the air after prey. The falcon was not allowed to eat the birds it caught. When the hunting day was over, it was rewarded with food and then allowed to fly free for a time.

Hunters wore a long, thick glove that the bird perched on. The birds were hooded when not hunting because it kept them calm.

Do ◆ Discuss ◆ Discover

1. a) Look up "ballad" in the dictionary. Write a description in your Vocabulary section.

   b) Discuss with a partner why ballads were a popular form of entertainment. Put main ideas in your notes.

A Medieval Christmas

O come and listen to my song
Of Christmas time in days far gone.
Meet the royal courtiers, the King and Queen,
At the finest spectacle you have seen.

From Nicholas Day to Epiphany
Dressed up in festive finery
The grandest nobles in the court
Will celebrate with merry sport.

Each day brave knights and ladies fair
On prancing chargers will gather there.
The clashing swords and banners bright
At tournaments will bring delight.

They'll eat the lavish festive feast
And watch St. George combat the beast.
Mummers and dancers all parade
In motley costumes and masquerade.

On Christmas Eve and Christmas morn
They'll kneel to greet the Christ child born.
And sing the angels' song of joy
To hail the birth of the holy Boy.

Then banquet, gifts, and good wassail,
With minstrels, jugglers and a funny tale
From the jester, who teases the noble folk
With skipping rhymes and many a joke.

So, all join hands and turn about,
Salute your partner with a shout,
And call a greeting of holiday cheer
For a Merry Christmas
and happy New Year!

—B. Gibbs

Gifts between kings could be very costly. In 1236, Henry III of England received a live elephant from the king of France!

The Christmas festivities began at St. Nicholas's Day (December 6) and ended at Epiphany (January 6). Hunting, tournaments, and lavish banquets were all part of the holiday.

Plays about St. George and the Dragon were especially popular at court at Christmas time.

Church and Kingdom

Leaders of the Church played important roles during medieval times. They often acted as royal advisors. However, they put the needs of the Church first. Church leaders and kings sometimes disagreed about power, money, and decisions that affected the kingdom.

Henry II and Becket

King Henry II and a noble named Thomas à Becket were good friends for many years. They hunted together and entertained each other. The king even sent one of his sons to be a page in Becket's household.

King Henry appointed Becket to the most important Church position in England, Archbishop of Canterbury. He was surprised when Becket suddenly became very religious. Becket refused to agree to changes King Henry wanted.

At that time, the Church had separate law courts from the king's court. If Church people broke the law, they were tried only in the Church court. King Henry wanted to change that. He had violent quarrels with Becket.

Some of Henry's knights overheard him ask why no one would free him of this troublesome bishop. One night in 1170, four of Henry's knights killed Thomas à Becket in the cathedral at Canterbury.

Everyone was shocked at this, including King Henry. The pope cast the king out of the Church. The churches of England were closed for a number of years. Henry had to do penance. He was forced to make a public display of his guilt and regret before the pope would pardon him.

Two years later, Thomas à Becket was declared to be a saint. Canterbury became a favourite destination for pilgrims who wanted to visit his shrine.

This container holds a relic of Saint Thomas à Becket.

Using Your Learning

Understanding Concepts

1. Make a web in your notes like the one shown below. Complete the web to show how religion was an important part of court life. Add more parts to the web as needed.

2. Choose any aspect of life at court and write a set of T-notes in your notes. Try to include at least 3 sub-topics.

3. Identify vocabulary from Chapter 8 to add to the Vocabulary section of your notebook. Add diagrams or sketches to help you remember the words and their meanings.

Developing Inquiry/Research and Communication Skills

4. Using the library and/or the Internet, research any king or queen of England who reigned between 1000 and 1400. Make notes of your findings. The website www.royal.gov.uk (go to Kids' Zone) may be useful.

Applying Skills and Concepts in Various Contexts

5. Locate and read a copy of the nursery rhyme "Sing a Song of Six Pence." Look at the food part of page 105 again. Draw a picture of the pie opening. What do you think about the custom of presenting live birds covered over with a pie crust? Would this be done today? Why or why not?

Medieval Times Project

1. As a group, create an assessment sheet for deciding whether the test version of the game was successful. Your criteria could include the following: Is the game fun? Will it help players learn? Are the length of playing time, level of difficulty, and fairness appropriate?

2. Have each member assess the test game using the sheet, then discuss the results. Decide on any changes to make to the design of the board, the way you use the information from the chapters, and the instructions for the game.

3. Identify key information about the life at court from Chapter 8. Use the form you have chosen and include it in the game.

Chapter 9
The Crusades

A series of wars about religion called the **Crusades** (1095–1291) brought many changes to people's lives. The Crusades had a huge cost in human lives and money. However, some Europeans also learned valuable things about the way of life in the Middle East. New ideas and products were exchanged that are part of our lives today.

Focus on Learning

In this chapter you will learn about
- the Holy Land
- Islamic culture in medieval times
- the Crusades
- Saladin and Richard I
- making a timeline
- effects of the Crusades

Vocabulary

Crusades
Holy Land
mosque

Qur'an
calligraphy

The Holy Land

Judaism (the Jewish religion), Christianity, and Islam all had their origins in the Middle East. Some places are considered holy by all three groups. In medieval times, this region was often called the Holy Land.

Much of the land was hot desert, rocky hills, and mountains. In some places, the land was fertile. If there was water, crops grew well. Most farming occurred in river valleys, along the seacoast, and around wells and springs. Most of the people lived in villages, towns, and cities. Some cities were large and wealthy because of trade.

The hot, dry environment in the Holy Land was completely different from the cooler, damper environment of most of Europe.

Jerusalem

The city of Jerusalem is important to all three religions today, just as in medieval times. (Jerusalem is in modern-day Israel.) Christians believe that Jesus was killed and then rose from the dead in Jerusalem. The Great Temple of Solomon, the Jewish central place of worship, once stood there. Muslims believe that the Prophet Mohammed rose to heaven in Jerusalem.

Many medieval Christians thought a pilgrimage to Jerusalem was the most important journey of their lives. (On page 60 you read about reasons people went on pilgrimages.)

The Dome of the Rock **mosque** (a Muslim religious building) stands where Mohammed is said to have gone up to heaven.

The Western Wall is all that remains in Jerusalem of the Jewish Great Temple.

Do ◊ Discuss ◊ Discover

1. Look at the map on page 30. Draw a sketch map in your notes showing the location of Jerusalem.

Islam

The founder of Islam was the Prophet Mohammed. He was born in what is now Saudi Arabia in 570. He wrote down the words that Allah (the God of Islam) revealed to him. These writings became the holy book of Islam called the Qur'an (Koran). The Prophet began teaching in Mecca. The first Islamic community was started in Medina. These are still holy places for followers of Islam.

Over the next 100 years, Muslim leaders took over large areas of land. Islam spread over a huge area. Different branches of the religion developed, but the basic beliefs remained the same.

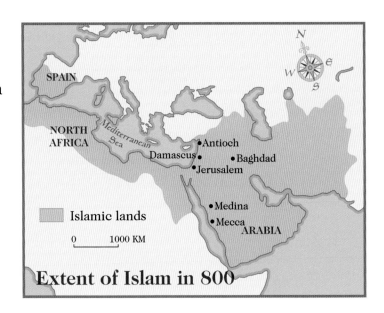

Extent of Islam in 800

Islamic lands

0 _____ 1000 KM

The Five Pillars of Islam

The religious duties of Muslims include the following five things:

1. to believe that there is no god but Allah, and Mohammed is his messenger

2. to pray five times each day facing Mecca

3. to fast (not eat or drink from dawn to dark) during the month of Ramadan each year

4. to give alms to the poor

5. to perform a pilgrimage to Mecca at least once

Legacy

Mosques are found all over the world where Muslim people live. They are usually built of local building materials. Mosques usually have a minaret, or tall tower, from which the people are called to prayer. There is a place inside with running water where people wash as they prepare to pray. A niche (hollow space) is built into the wall that faces the holy city of Mecca. People stand or kneel in rows facing the niche when they pray.

This modern mosque is in Toronto.

Life in the Holy Land

Houses

Houses in the Holy Land had thick, outer walls and cool, central courtyards. Gardens often had fountains or running water flowing among trees and flowers.

Men and women lived in separate parts of the house. Carpets and pillows made comfortable places to eat, talk, play games such as chess, recite poetry, and listen to music.

Food and Drink

Cherries, figs, dates, grapes, strawberries, oranges, lemons, apricots, and peaches were among the many kinds of fruit grown. Grain was grown to make flour for bread. Fish, legumes, and some kinds of meat such as lamb were eaten. Pork was forbidden by the Qur'an.

Sugar cane was a crop that became a source of wealth from trade. Oil pressed from olives was used for cooking, burning in oil lamps for light, and making soap.

Sherbet and cool drinks were made from snow brought from distant mountains. Drinks were made from fruit juice and honey or from grains. Wine and alcohol were forbidden.

Clothing

Both men and women wore layers of loose, flowing clothing. Head coverings protected them from the sun. Women wore veils that covered their hair and most of their faces when they were away from home.

Clothing was made of cotton, silk, wool, and linen. Muslim traders originally imported silk and cotton from China and India. By medieval times, silk and cotton were being produced in the Middle East and exported to Europe. Slipper-like shoes were made of soft leather or cloth.

Do ◊ Discuss ◊ Discover

1. Choose a graphic organizer to compare life in the Holy Land with life in a castle as it is described in Chapter 4.

Ideas and Technology

At the time of the Crusades, science, technology, mathematics, and medicine were much more advanced in Islamic countries than in Europe. There were large libraries of written works in Islamic cities. Education and ideas were very important.

Muslim scholars were interested in many kinds of knowledge. They preserved and translated written works of the ancient Greeks and other groups from the past. Most of these writings were unknown in Europe. Many ancient Greek writings are known and taught everywhere today because Islamic scholars studied them.

As Islam spread, new ideas and products were adopted. They were traded with other regions. When Muslim traders visited other lands, they brought back both products and ideas. For example, the numerals we use today were brought from India by Muslim scribes.

The sextant and astrolabe were developed by Muslim astronomers, who studied the stars. Travellers used them to figure out their location from the angles of the stars and sun. This made travel by sea and land much safer.

The Arts

Showing humans or animals in Islamic religious art was forbidden. Muslim artists developed a style that used geometric shapes, vegetation, and **calligraphy**. Calligraphy is an artistic form of writing or lettering.

Sayings from the Qur'an were used to decorate buildings and objects such as dishes. Illuminations were made on parchment scrolls and in books. Coloured tiles in geometric patterns were often used to decorate buildings.

These Muslim astronomers are using dividers, triangles, a tool to measure angles, a sextant, rulers, a globe, and an hourglass.

Do ♦ Discuss ♦ Discover

1. As a class, develop 5 questions to assist in researching the sextant and astrolabe. (You do not have to carry out this research.)

The Crusades

The Holy Land and much of the area around it was controlled by Muslim peoples. Pilgrims travelled through these lands on their way to Jerusalem and other holy places.

About 1050, an Islamic group called the Seljuk Turks took over the region. They did not permit Christian pilgrims to enter their territory.

In 1095, Pope Urban II called to Christian kings, knights, and soldiers to take the Holy Land away from the Turks. European rulers, the Church, and others had various reasons to support the pope. The pope expected other people to help pay for the war through taxes and gifts. People of all kinds answered the pope's appeal, for many different reasons.

A Monk
"I took a vow to obey the will of God when I became a monk. The Holy Father has said that God wills this Crusade, so I will go and do what I can."

A Trader
"The opportunities for trade are enormous. The Turks now control very valuable markets and products. I want to get some of that profit. This way of travelling is as safe as any other."

A Blacksmith
"I don't want to spend my whole life in a village making horseshoes. My skills are needed by the army. I will see all sorts of new places. Perhaps I will also take home riches when we are victorious."

A Mason and His Wife
"His Holiness the Pope has promised forgiveness for our sins if we go on a Crusade. We will be assured of a place in heaven when we die."

A huge number of ordinary people started out before the armies of the first Crusade were ready to leave. Most had too little money and food. They starved, stole from local people, and were attacked by bandits and armed forces along the way. Most did not complete the journey.

Over the next 200 years, a number of Crusades took place. Both the Crusaders and Muslims won and lost territory. Thousands of Christians, Muslims, and Jews died or were killed during the Crusades.

The First Crusade

Several armies followed different routes to the Holy Land to fight in the First Crusade. They suffered terribly on the journey. The men and horses were not used to the hot climate of the Middle East. When horses died, knights had to walk and carry or drag their heavy metal armour.

A Lady
"My husband said he would be away for more than a year. I want to be by my husband's side and help take back the Holy Land. My husband's brother will stay on our land."

A Knight
"My lord promised 50 knights and horses. It was my duty to come on this journey. Many have died from sickness and lack of food and water. There were accidents on the way and the river crossings were dangerous. Now we must face the enemy when we are exhausted."

A Potter
"One reason I joined the Crusade was to come and see the remarkable pottery and tiles made here. I want to learn new skills. Everyone will want my work, and it will bring high prices when I get home."

A Lord
"This is a holy war to recover the sacred places where Christ lived and died. As Christian knights, we must take back the Holy Land and make these places safe for pilgrims again."

In 1099, about 1000 knights and 10 000 other soldiers fought a number of battles and captured a large area of the Holy Land, including Jerusalem.

The sieges and battles were terrible. There was little mercy shown to people living in the captured cities. Thousands of ordinary people were killed. There was great violence and cruelty. Soldiers and knights looted mosques, businesses, and homes to steal anything of value.

Europeans captured and held parts of the Middle East for about 200 years. They built castles and churches and settled among the Muslim peoples. While they lived there, they adopted some parts of the way of life. European Crusaders who returned to Europe brought with them new ideas and the taste for new products.

Do ◆ Discuss ◆ Discover

1. Review pages 117 and 118 and summarize in your notes the different reasons people participated in the Crusades.

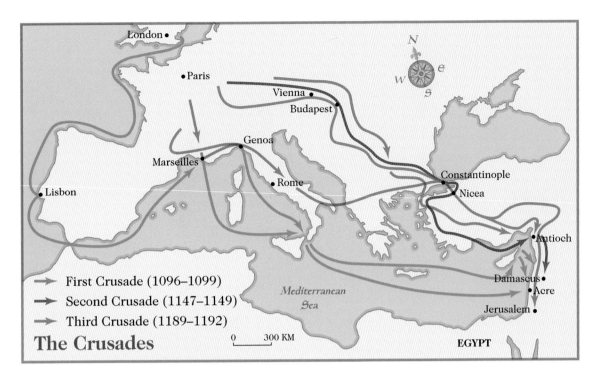

The Crusades

First Crusade (1096–1099)
Second Crusade (1147–1149)
Third Crusade (1189–1192)

0 ___ 300 KM

Mediterranean Sea

EGYPT

Islamic Opposition

Gradually, the Islamic forces recovered from their defeat in the First Crusade. In 1144, they recaptured some land.

European Christians began the Second Crusade to help defend the Holy Land in 1147. It ended in 1149.

In 1169, a strong Muslim leader called Saladin became ruler of Egypt. Over the next 18 years, Saladin's armies captured Crusader castles and took back more lands. When Saladin recaptured Jerusalem in 1187, the pope quickly called for another Crusade.

The Third Crusade

The Third Crusade is sometimes called the Crusade of the Kings. Both Richard I of England and Philip II of France led armies that travelled by sea to the Holy Land. The huge army of the German ruler travelled overland. Unfortunately, when their leader drowned, many of his troops returned home.

The Crusaders recaptured the city of Acre in 1191. Philip and his army returned to Europe, and Richard's army marched on. After fighting several more battles, Richard realized they would never capture Jerusalem. Richard and Saladin agreed to a truce. The terms allowed Christian pilgrims to visit Jerusalem.

The Christian forces held most of the coast for another hundred years. The last stronghold, at Acre, was lost in 1291.

Saladin (1137–1193)

Salah-ed-din Yussuf (Saladin) came from a military family. He was an army general who rose to power through his great abilities. He became ruler of Egypt in 1169 and ruler of Syria in 1174. The alliances he made between different Islamic groups helped defeat the Christians in the Holy Land.

If necessary, Saladin would crush an enemy without mercy to meet his military goals. However, he was known to be chivalrous and honest by both his supporters and enemies.

For example, Saladin's forces greatly outnumbered the Crusaders in a battle in 1192. However, Richard's leadership was keeping the Crusaders from being overwhelmed. Suddenly, Richard's horse was killed. Richard was fighting bravely on foot, but he was in great danger. Saladin quickly sent horses to Richard's side, so he could choose one and remount. This was an example of his respect for Richard's ability as a leader.

Saladin died the year after the truce was signed.

Richard I (1157–1199)

Richard I was a son of King Henry II of England and Eleanor of Aquitaine. He was educated in France and became Duke of Aquitaine in 1172.

When his father died in 1189, Richard was crowned King of England. After his coronation, he began to raise money and troops to go on a Crusade. He left his mother to rule England with his royal advisors.

Although Richard was a brave military leader, he quarrelled with other Christian leaders. This led him into difficulties. When he was returning to Europe in 1192, after making the truce with Saladin, he was captured by the Duke of Austria. The German ruler then held him for ransom. Eleanor had to raise 150 000 marks (millions of dollars today) to pay for his release.

After he was released in 1194, Richard returned to England. He raised more money for his army and returned to France.

Richard died in France in 1199 after being hit by a crossbow bolt.

Timelines

A timeline is a graphic organizer. Timelines display information about events in the order they occurred.

Timelines can include numbers, words, and pictures. They can be designed horizontally, vertically, or in a shape. For example, you could make a timeline of the Crusades on a picture of a long banner.

To create a timeline, follow the steps below:

1. List the events you wish to include, with the date each occurred.

2. Put the events in sequence by date, beginning with the earliest.

3. Decide on the start and end points of the period your timeline must cover.

4. Divide your timeline into equal steps (intervals). These intervals represent periods of time. You will need enough room in each to write in an event or make a sketch.

5. Make a rough sketch of your timeline. Put the earliest and latest dates on it. Figure out where the other dates fit in between them. Label each of the events.

6. If you do an illustrated timeline, decide how you would like to illustrate it. You might

   • put a symbol or image beside the major events

   • decorate the borders or the blank part of your page

7. Draw, label, and illustrate your finished timeline. Add a title for the timeline that includes the time period shown; for example, "Richard I *Coeur de Lion*, 1157–1199."

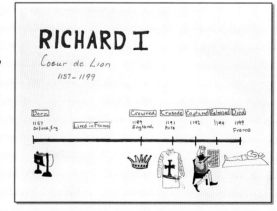

Do ◊ Discuss ◊ Discover

1. Using the steps listed above, make a timeline of your life so far.

121

Effects of the Crusades

Christians and Muslims were in contact for a long time during the Crusades. This contact changed life in both Europe and the Middle East in many ways. Thousands of lives were lost on both sides. The financial costs were also enormous.

Contact with Islam during the Crusades and in later years changed life in Europe in other ways. The chart below shows some examples.

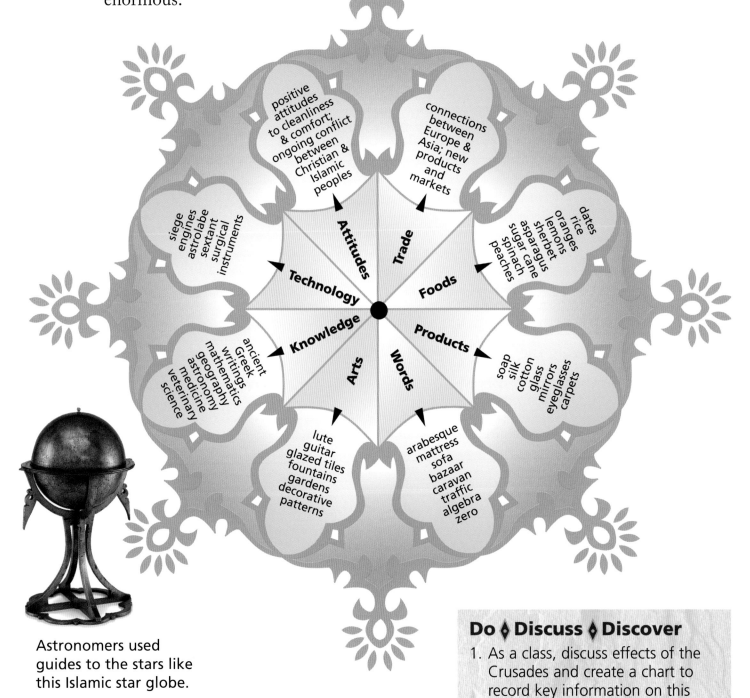

Attitudes: positive attitudes to cleanliness & comfort; ongoing conflict between Christian & Islamic peoples

Trade: connections between Europe & Asia; new products and markets

Foods: dates, rice, oranges, lemons, sherbet, asparagus, sugar cane, spinach, peaches

Technology: siege engines, astrolabe, sextant, surgical instruments

Products: soap, silk, cotton, glass, mirrors, eyeglasses, carpets

Knowledge: ancient Greek writings, mathematics, geography, astronomy, medicine, veterinary science

Arts: lute, guitar, glazed tiles, fountains, gardens, decorative patterns

Words: arabesque, mattress, sofa, bazaar, caravan, traffic, algebra, zero

Astronomers used guides to the stars like this Islamic star globe.

Do ◊ Discuss ◊ Discover

1. As a class, discuss effects of the Crusades and create a chart to record key information on this topic for your notebooks.

Using Your Learning

Understanding Concepts

1. Record in your notebook the challenges faced by people involved in the Crusades.

2. Make a web in your notes like the one shown below. Complete the web to show different aspects of Islamic life. Add more parts to the web as needed.

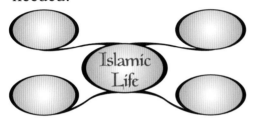

Islamic Life

3. Identify vocabulary from Chapter 9 to add to the Vocabulary section of your notebook. Add diagrams or sketches to help you remember the words and their meanings.

Developing Inquiry/Research and Communication Skills

4. Research different styles of calligraphy using library resources and the Internet. Choose a calligraphic style to write your name, the name of your pet, or a favourite character or hero. Display your work.

Applying Skills and Concepts in Various Contexts

5. Write a ballad about a figure from the Crusades describing his or her heroic deeds.

6. New ideas and technology are often developed in one country and borrowed or adopted in many other places. The names or words describing them are often also adopted. For example, the lute and its name both came from Islam. Use a dictionary or the Internet to find three more examples of words used in English that were adopted at the same time as a piece of technology or a new idea. They do not have to be from medieval times.

Medieval Times Project

1. Assign tasks for constructing the final game board, making or collecting the final game materials, and writing out the revised instructions.

2. Discuss a design for the box or packaging for your game.

3. Identify key information about the Crusades from Chapter 9. Use the form you have chosen to include it in the game.

Chapter 10
Travel and Trade

During the Crusades, the number of people travelling increased. Armies, pilgrims, and traders travelled across Europe and around the coast by seacoast. Contact with other places brought new ideas and goods. It also helped a terrible disease spread across Asia and Europe in the 1300s. Changes in society began to happen more quickly.

Focus on Learning

In this chapter you will learn about
- travelling and trade
- trade routes and products
- a disease called the plague
- effects of the plague

Vocabulary

courier	last rites
plague	revolt
bubonic	

Travel and Trade

In early medieval times, most people travelled on foot or horseback. There were few roads that could carry wagons. Goods were carried on pack horses, mules, and donkeys. Many goods were also transported by river.

Gradually, more roads were built. In wet weather, roads were often too muddy for wagons to use. Villages were expected to maintain the roads near them.

Heavier, bulkier loads of goods were carried by ship. New technology like the compass and the astrolabe helped ship captains find their way without getting lost. Bad weather, sharp underwater rocks, and pirates were all dangers for sea travellers.

Traders travelled most of the year. They bought goods in one place to sell in another. They travelled to large seasonal fairs in different places to buy and sell goods.

The business of trade was risky. There was danger from accidents and thieves. Products could be damaged. They might spoil before they were sold.

At night, travelling nobles stayed in castles or manor houses. Merchants stayed in inns, the poor looked for a monastery, and the poorest slept outside.

Although there were risks, many traders became wealthy. Large profits could be made from imported goods, such as spices from Asia. Essential goods, such as metals, grain, and wool, were also profitable.

Legacy

Modern banking had its beginnings in medieval times. Medieval merchants and traders used written letters of credit that guaranteed that bills would be paid. This meant traders did not have to carry huge sums in gold and silver coins with them.

Trade Routes

In spite of the dangers and difficulties, regular trade routes connected many places in Europe, and linked Europe with Asia.

Important letters were carried by **couriers**, as there was no mail system. A person wanting to send a letter looked for a traveller going to that town.

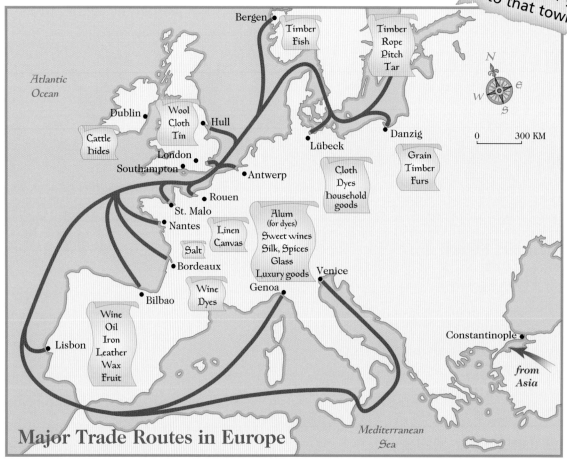

Major Trade Routes in Europe

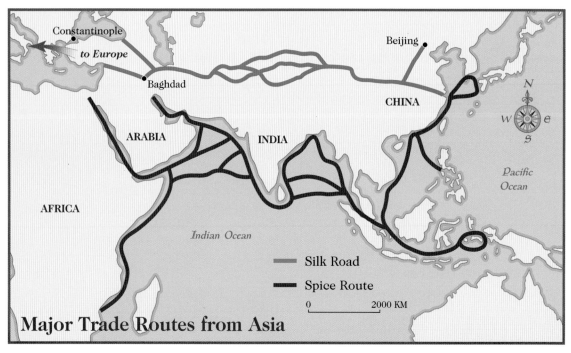

Major Trade Routes from Asia

Marco Polo

Marco Polo was a member of a trading family from Venice (Italy). Venice had a huge ship-building industry. Wealthy merchants from Venice had fleets of trading ships. Much of the trade from the Middle East and Asia reached Europe through Venice and other Italian cities.

Marco Polo wrote a book about the trip he made to China. He travelled with his two uncles, long before other Europeans went there. They reached Beijing in 1278. The ruler of China, Kublai Khan, allowed the Polo family to travel safely anywhere in China. Marco Polo wrote about China's government, shipping, roads, canal systems, cities, and technology.

Trade with Asia

The most famous land trade route across Asia was called the Silk Road. It was thousands of kilometres long. It stretched across high mountains and huge deserts, from the Mediterranean Sea to Beijing. Camel caravans carried goods along the Silk Road.

Trade with China during the medieval period was largely by sea. Muslim traders controlled the price of goods from Asia. They transported goods from India and China across the Middle East. There, they sold them to European traders. Some Europeans wanted to deal directly with Asian traders. For a time in the late-1200s, the Polo family and some other European traders were able to trade directly with China.

Do ◊ Discuss ◊ Discover

1. Write your own caption for either illustration on this page. Share it with a classmate.

The Plague

In the 1300s, traders began to hear stories of a terrible sickness in Asia. They heard that up to half of the population in China might have died.

A **plague** is a dangerous disease that spreads rapidly from one person to another. Each year, plague outbreaks occurred nearer England. The map below shows how the plague spread across Europe.

The Black Death

The plague that swept across Asia and Europe in the 1300s had several different forms. The name Black Death came from the **bubonic** form of the plague.

The bacteria that caused the bubonic plague were transmitted by fleas on rats. When the fleas left an infected rat and bit a person, the bacteria entered the person's bloodstream. Then the person got the plague.

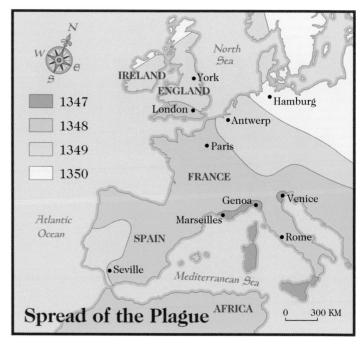

People with bubonic plague developed painful, swollen black lumps in their armpits about two weeks after being infected. They ran a high fever and vomited. Most died within five to seven days.

Outbreaks of bubonic plague often slowed down or stopped in winter. Cold weather killed the fleas, and people travelled less.

Another form of plague, called the pneumonic plague, affected the sick person's lungs. It was spread through the air by coughing. Sick people died even more quickly than with the bubonic plague, usually within a day or two.

Some people did not get sick, even though they were in contact with sick people. A small number of people who caught the plague recovered.

Spread of the Plague

The plague spread from seaports and places along the Silk Road. Travellers and rats on ships carried it from one place to the next.

Fighting the Plague

People in medieval times did not understand about germs and bacteria. However, they did understand that diseases could be contagious—that is, people could get a disease from being in contact with other sick people.

Most people thought that the illness was caused by dirty or smelly, poisoned air. Some doctors wore leather masks with a bird-like beak over their noses when they treated the sick. People held perfumed cloths or bunches of spices or herbs in front of their faces to sweeten the air. In 1349, King Edward III ordered the Lord Mayor of London to make people clean up the filthy streets. He thought the plague was spread by smells.

People were terrified of the plague. Many left the towns and cities to avoid it. However, if they were already infected, they carried the disease with them and it spread farther.

Many people bravely nursed sick family and community members. Some priests prayed for the sick and performed the ceremony of **last rites** for them when they died. Some monasteries and convents took in the sick and fed orphans whose families had died. Other people, including Church people, were so frightened they refused to give aid of any kind. Huge numbers of people of all kinds became infected and died.

The first people to die received funerals and were buried with the normal rites. Soon, so many were sick and so many had died that the dead were buried in mass graves with no ceremony at all.

Out of a total population of approximately 100 000 people in London, about 30 000 died of the plague in 1348 and 1349.

Do ◊ Discuss ◊ Discover

1. Review page 100. Begin a Cause and Effect organizer of causes and effects of the plague. Fill in the sections for Causes and Event. Put it in your notebook. You will complete it on page 131.

A Visitor

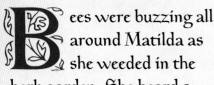

Bees were buzzing all around Matilda as she weeded in the herb garden. She heard a sound and looked up. A thin, dusty boy stood outside her mother's gate. He seemed to hesitate. "Hello," he said. "Does the sister of David Cotter of London live here?"

The boy had a cloth bundle held by a strap slung over his shoulder. A short dagger hung from his belt. Matilda stood up and faced him. Travellers were not welcome. Their village was still untouched by the plague. She wondered who he was, to know the name of her uncle. "Who are you?" she asked loudly. "You cannot come here if you have been where there is plague."

Matilda's mother came out of the house. "It is Hugh, is it not?" Her round face was filled with alarm. "But, you are alone. Has something happened to David and Magda and your brothers?" She stopped short before she reached him.

The boy's voice was husky with sadness. "They have all died of the plague, Aunt. I didn't know what to do. I took what food and money I could find and left. I stayed

away from towns and villages. I have been walking for nine days, and I'm tired, but I'm not sick. Please, Aunt, I will show you." He pulled off his shirt and held up his arms, showing his aunt his thin body.

Matilda's mother went closer and looked for signs of the black swellings of plague, but there were none. She reached out to feel his forehead for signs of fever, but his tired face was cool. "Oh, Hugh!" she cried, with tears on her face. She reached over the gate to put her arms around him. "I am sorry to be so cautious. I was afraid for my own children. Poor child, come to the house."

She swung the gate open, still talking.

"Matilda, come greet your cousin. Then bring water from the well so Hugh can wash off the dust. Hugh, you must rest first.

"After the meal tonight you will tell us what you have seen. I must learn everything you know, because if the sickness comes here I will have to do what I can to help people. What treatments do the doctors use? Do you know why so many died and you have survived? Do you know of herbs that may help? Please, don't say that the doctors bleed them. I won't do that…." She drew the boy gently into the house.

Effects of the Plague

In 1348 and 1349 in England, about one-third of the people died. Crops were not harvested and animals were not fed or cared for. There was a severe shortage of food in some places.

Some villages were deserted when the survivors moved to other villages or better land. On some manors, farm fields were turned into pasture for animals because there were too few workers.

Trade slowed down. Cities closed their gates against travellers, and harbours would not allow ships to dock.

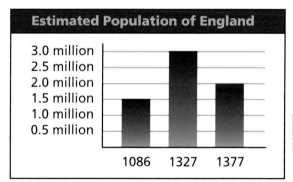

Estimated Population of England

	1086	1327	1377

(3.0 million, 2.5 million, 2.0 million, 1.5 million, 1.0 million, 0.5 million)

Workers and Wages

Medieval society had already begun to change before the plague brought even larger changes. By the mid-1300s, many serfs and villagers paid rent for their land and houses rather than giving hours of labour on the lord's fields. Manors paid more workers a day-wage rather than providing them with a house and land in return for work. More villagers moved to towns.

After the plague killed so many people, there were too few workers left. Workers wanted higher wages. If a lord wanted his grain harvested, he had to pay more. However, the value of products was lower because trade slowed down. There were fewer people, so there was less demand for products. Some lords could not afford higher wages.

There was a royal proclamation that workers had to continue to work for the old rate of pay. This made them angry. In 1381, in the south and east parts of England, rural working people rose up in **revolt**. There were several clashes between workers and authorities. However, the revolt was quickly put down.

Do ◊ Discuss ◊ Discover

1. Finish the Cause and Effect organizer you started on page 129.

Using Your Learning

Understanding Concepts

1. Based on what you now know about living conditions in medieval times, summarize in your notes why the plague spread so quickly and easily.

2. Locate the prediction chart you did on page 4. Complete your chart by filling in the third column. Compare this with your predictions. Share the chart with a classmate.

3. Identify vocabulary from Chapter 10 to add to the Vocabulary section of your notebook. Add diagrams or sketches to help you remember the words and their meanings.

Developing Inquiry/Research and Communication Skills

4. Imagine you are going to research the plague. Write out 4 questions you would want to find answers for in your research. (You do not need to carry out the research.)

5. Imagine you are a merchant coming to London to sell your goods. Create a poster advertising your product to put on your market stall at a fair.

6. Create an illustrated timeline of events in the medieval period. Look through the textbook and write down events and dates that will make your timeline interesting.

Applying Skills and Concepts in Various Contexts

7. In a group, discuss ways that contagious diseases are treated or prevented today. Compare this with medieval times.

Medieval Times Project

1. Identify key information about Travel and Trade from Chapter 10. Include it in your game in the form you have chosen.

2. Finish constructing the final board game, game materials, and packaging or box.

3. Soon you will be presenting your game to the class and taking part in a tournament of games. As a group, decide on the best way to present your game. Choose roles for the presentation.

Conclusion

Features of Medieval Life

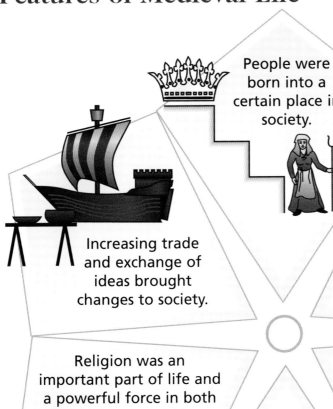

People were born into a certain place in society.

A few people held most of the power, wealth, and land.

Increasing trade and exchange of ideas brought changes to society.

Most people worked at producing food.

Religion was an important part of life and a powerful force in both Christendom and Islam.

It was a time of war and conflict over control of land.

Do ◊ Discuss ◊ Discover

1. Review the introduction and illustration on pages 2 and 3 of the textbook. Working in groups of three, discuss the ways that this page and the illustration on pages 2 and 3 summarize the main features of medieval life. You may wish to use a web to record your ideas.

Medieval Times Project

It is time for all of the groups in the class to share their Medieval Times games with each other. This activity will have two parts:

* presentation of games
* game tournament

Presentations

1. Each group has 5 minutes to present its game. Your group should display your game and then describe it. Say what type of game it is and what its parts are. Then give a general idea how it is played.

2. Describe what challenges the group faced in designing and constructing the game, and what you learned in the process.

Game Tournament

1. Your teacher will organize a time and place for the groups to play each other's games.

2. Afterwards, discuss the different games as a class. What features in other groups' games did you particularly like? What features of your own game did you like?

Glossary

A

abbey—a place where a religious community of monks or nuns lived

allegiance—a promise of loyalty and support to someone stronger

alliance—an agreement between groups benefitting all of them

alms—gifts of money, food, clothing, or shoes to poor people

apothecary—a person who made medicines to treat diseases

apprentice—a young person learning a trade from a master craftsperson

armoury—a place where armourers made and repaired armour and weapons

astrolabe—a tool for figuring out location based on the angles of the stars

astronomy—the study of the stars

B

bailiff—the lord's employee who supervised serfs' work, enforced the lord's laws, and oversaw a village

Bible—the holy book of Christianity

blacksmith—a craftsperson who made tools and metal objects and shoed horses

bloodletting—bleeding a patient to cure an illness

bubonic—a plague caused by bacteria spread by rat fleas, which caused high fever, painful black lumps, and death

buttress—a stone structure that strengthened the walls of a tall building

C

calligraphy—an artistic form of writing or lettering

carding—combing raw fleece to straighten the fibres so they could be spun into thread

cathedral—a large church in the centre of a Church region with a bishop at its head

chain mail—shirts, hoods, and leg coverings made of rows of interlocking metal rings

chamber—a room

chamber pot—a container used as a toilet, which had to be emptied

chapel—a small building or a room in a larger building, used for religious services or prayer

charter—a document signed by a king making a town independent from a lord

chivalry—the ways the perfect knight was expected to be and behave: brave, loyal, sincerely Christian, and protective of all women

Christianity—a religion based on the teachings of Jesus Christ; its followers, Christians, believe in one God in three persons (Father, Son, Holy Spirit)

common—shared land used as pasture by the villagers, not used by the lord

conquer—to take control of a place by defeating the defenders in war

consensus—a way of making decisions in which everyone has to agree on a solution before it is accepted

contagious—a disease that can be caught through contact with a sick person

convent—a religious community of nuns

coronation—the ceremony in which a king or queen is crowned as ruler of a kingdom

courier—a person who is paid to deliver letters and packages

courtiers—members of noble families who stayed at the royal court as guests, ambassadors, ladies-in-waiting, and knights

Crusades—a series of wars about controlling the Holy Lands (1095–1291)

curfew—the time after which everyone was supposed to be home in bed, when the town gates were locked

curtain wall—a fortified stone wall around a castle complex

D

distaff—a rod used for twisting thread

document—an official piece of writing

Domesday Book—a large book in which officials of King William I recorded information about everything everyone in England owned

drawbridge—a bridge over the moat that could be raised to keep people out of a castle

E

exchequer—a system of checking taxes collected for the royal treasury, originally using a checkered cloth

F

fair—a large gathering where products were bought and sold, held seasonally in specific towns and cities

falconry—a sport using trained hawks or falcons to hunt birds and small animals

fallow—a field in which no crop was grown for a year so the soil could rest

ford—a shallow place in a river where people and animals could cross

forge—a structure holding the hot fire used by a blacksmith for heating metal

freemen, freewomen—workers who were paid for their work and paid rent for their houses

fuller—a person who ran a fulling mill, where new woolen cloth was cleaned and pounded to make it warmer and more waterproof

G

garderobe—a toilet built into a wall, which emptied into a cesspit below

Gothic—a style of architecture that featured pointed arches over doors and windows, and tall, slim columns

great hall—a large room in a manor house or castle used for banquets, meetings, and special events

guild—an organization of workers of a certain craft or merchants selling a certain product, which looked after the interests of its members

H

healer—a person who used herbal remedies to help sick or injured people

heir—someone who receives a person's possessions when the person dies

heraldry—a system of symbols used on coats of arms representing noble families

high table—table on a raised platform in the great hall where the lord and his most important guests sat

Holy Land—a region of the Middle East considered holy by Jewish, Christian, and Muslim people

hospice—an early type of hospital started by religious communities to look after pilgrims and elderly, needy, and sick people

I

illumination—tiny illustrations in the initial capital letter on a page and other decorations in hand-made medieval books

inherit—to receive something from someone who has died

Islam—a religion that had its beginnings in the writings and teachings of the Prophet Mohammed; its followers, known as Muslims, believe in one God (Allah)

J

Jerusalem—a city (in modern-day Israel) considered holy by Jewish, Christian, and Muslim peoples

jester—an entertainer who performed comedy

joiner—a woodworker who built and repaired carts, furniture, and wooden objects

journeyman—a craftsperson who had finished training and travelled from job to job working by the day

jousting—a competition in which two knights on horseback tried to knock each other down with their long lances

Judaism—the religion of the Jewish people, who believe in one God (Yahweh)

K

keep—a tower several stories high, usually surrounded by a high wall

kingdom—all of the land governed by a king and his vassals

knight—a medieval European warrior, usually from a noble family, who fought on horseback

L

lady-in-waiting—a woman from a noble family who served another noble lady as companion and helper

last rites—a ceremony performed by a priest for a dying person

latrine—an outdoor toilet or outhouse

linen—cloth woven from fibres in the stem of the flax plant

M

Magna Carta—the charter signed by King John that limited the power of rulers to make decisions without consulting their subjects

malnutrition—not having enough of the right kinds of food to eat

manor—lands given by a ruler to a noble or knight to provide his income

manorial court—place where the lord or his representative heard complaints and judged legal cases involving people from the manor

market—a gathering at which people sold or exchanged mainly locally produced farm products

mason—a craftsperson who cut, shaped, and built structures from stone

meadow—a field in which long grass was cut to make hay

merchant—a business person who bought, sold, and traded goods

miller—a person who operated a water mill or windmill to grind grain into flour

minaret—a tall tower from which followers of Islam are called to prayer

minstrel—a singer and musician who entertained for pay

moat—a ditch filled with water around the base of a castle wall, which helped keep attackers away from the walls

monastery—a religious community of monks

mosque—a religious building used by Muslims for prayer, community meetings, and teaching

motte and bailey—a wooden tower surrounded by a wall on top of a mound of earth (motte) with a fenced area (bailey) at the base of the hill

mummers—serfs and freemen wearing masks who put on skits and mimes in return for gifts of food and pennies

Muslim—a follower of the Islamic religion

N

night watch—guards that patrolled town streets at night

nobles—the most important and powerful families

O

open field system—method of separating strips of land with a track or furrow instead of a fence or hedge

P

page—a boy from a noble family who served and did errands for a lord and lady in another noble household while being educated

parchment—thin, smooth, dry animal skin used for writing on

pasture—field where animals were fed on grass

penance—an activity that people had to perform to show they regretted their wrong-doings

petition—a written request to an authority asking for a change

pilgrim—a traveller who went on a journey to visit a holy place

plague—a dangerous, contagious disease

poacher—a person who hunted or fished illegally

portcullis—a strong gate at the castle entrance that could be raised and lowered

proclamation—an important public message that affected everybody, announced by a town crier or an official

Q

Qur'an—(Koran) the holy book of Islam, based on the writings and teachings of the Prophet Mohammed

R

ransom—a sum of money demanded for the safe return of a captured prisoner

reeve—a villager who organized village work and acted as foreman

regent—someone who ruled on behalf of a king or queen who was a child or absent from the kingdom

relic—a religious object such as a bone or a possession of a saint believed to have special powers

revolt—an uprising against those in authority in order to cause change

Romanesque—a style of architecture (building) featuring rounded arches over doors and windows, thick stone walls, and thick pillars

royal court—the king's court; the king, his advisors, and trusted officials, who governed the kingdom; also, the place where the ruler lived and met with people

S

sanitation—methods of protecting health through cleanliness and disposing of sewage and garbage

self-sufficient—able to meet basic needs for food, shelter, and clothing without help from elsewhere

serf—farm workers who worked nobles' land in return for a place to live and the right to use some land for their own income

sheriff—a noble who acted as an official of the king, enforcing the king's laws, and collecting taxes for a town or a region

shrine—a place where people went to pray, built somewhere thought to be holy

siege—surrounding a castle and preventing supplies of food and water from reaching it to force the people inside to surrender

society—all of the people of a place at a certain time

solar—a room in a castle or house used as a private area for the family and personal servants

squire—a noble youth who was training to be a knight in another noble's household

staple foods—basic foods eaten every day

starvation—not having enough to eat

steward—the lord's official who acted as a business manager

stocks—a wooden frame set up in a public place that held prisoners by their ankles so others could criticize or throw rotten food at them

stonemason—a craftsperson who cut and shaped stone, and built stone structures

surcoat—a garment worn over a long shirt or underdress

T

technology—tools and ideas for solving problems

thatched roof—a roof made of thick layers of bundles of straw or reeds tied onto a wooden roof frame

tithe—a percentage of a person's income or goods, usually one tenth, given to support the work of the Church

tournament—competition in which knights got practice in combat skills

town council—a group of townspeople who made many decisions about how a town was run

trencher—a thick piece of old bread used as a plate

troubadour—a poet who sang and recited poetry about chivalry and love

V

vassal—someone who promised loyalty and some services to someone more powerful in return for some land and the income it produced

vow—a solemn promise

W

warhorse—a knight's strong, aggressive horse that was trained to withstand battle conditions

wattle and daub—thin branches woven together between support beams, plastered with a mixture of clay, dung, and straw; used to make walls of houses

weaver—a craftsperson who made cloth from thread

Index

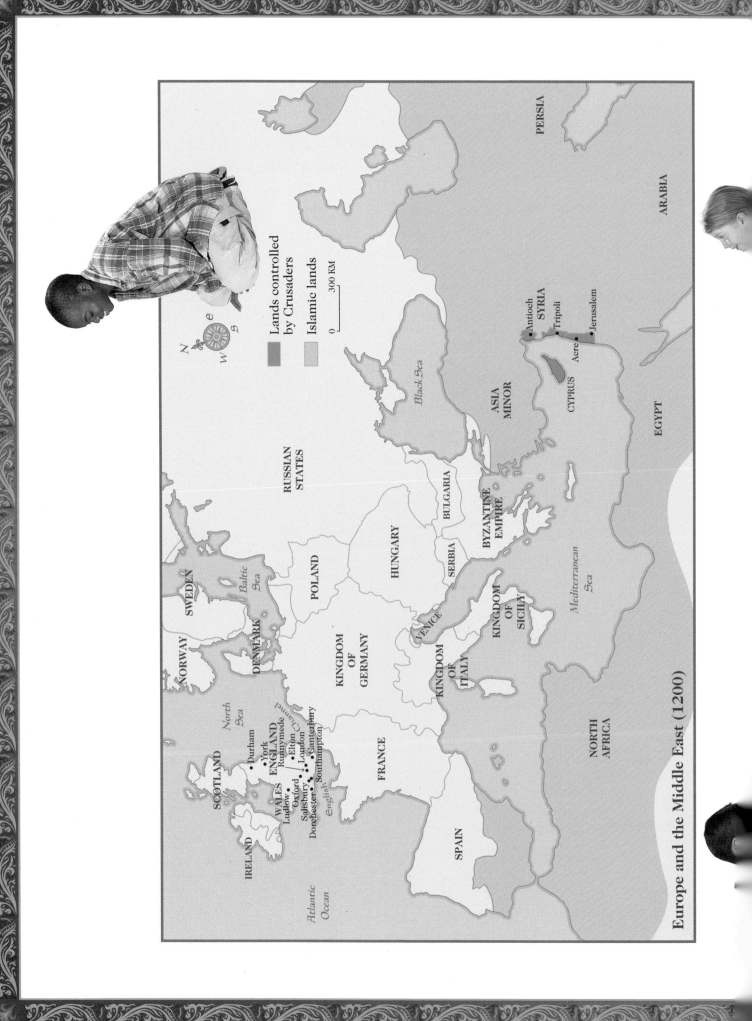

Europe and the Middle East (1200)